Ministry
for Social Crisis

Theology and Praxis
in the Black Church Tradition

Ministry for Social Crisis

Theology and Praxis in the Black Church Tradition

Forrest E. Harris, Sr.,

Mercer University Press
Macon, Georgia

ISBN 0-86554-429-8

Ministry for Social Crisis
Theology and Praxis in the Black Church Tradition

by Forrest E. Harris, Sr.,

Copyright © 1993
Mercer University Press

Printed in the United Sates of America.

The paper used in this publication meets the minimum requirements
of American National Standard for Information Sciences—
Permanence of Paper for Printed Library Materials,
ANSI Z39.48-1984.

Library of Congress Cataloging-in-Publication Data

Harris, Forrest E.
Ministry for social crisis : theology and praxis in the black church
tradition / by Forrest E. Harris, Sr.,
x + 142 pp.   6x9" (15x23 cm)
Includes bibliographical references and index.
ISBN 0-86554-429-8
1. Church and social problems—United States. 2. Sociology, Christian.
I. Title.
BR563.N4H36677 1993
261.8'089'96073—dc20   93-36038
CIP

Contents

To My Wife Jackie,
whose love brings grace and dignity
to me and our children
and
to the memory of
the Reverend Brady Johnson,
whose prophetic preaching
at Spring Hill Baptist Church,
Memphis, Tennessee,
gave the hope of liberation
to a host of ebony sons and daughters
for forty years

Preface

This project was inspired by the 1983 Lyman Beecher Lectures at Yale Divinity School, delivered by the late Kelly Miller Smith, Sr. These lectures, published under the title *Social Crisis Preaching*, show how preaching about social crisis serves a "prophetic" function in addressing racial and social oppression. Smith further argues that prophetic preaching is a form of social action and a force for producing social change. In Smith's view, then, prophetic proclamation and social action are undifferentiated. If preaching does not make a difference in the shape of the world, then it is a defective form of communication, according to Smith. He writes: "The impact of social crisis preaching has made the difference in slavery, the pursuit of social justice and peace."[1] Social crisis preaching, as defined by Smith, articulates a prophetic vision by which the African American community might become emancipated from social oppression. Moreover, the black church's prophetic preaching tradition and competence for social crisis ministry are inseparable elements for equipping that institution for sustained liberative ministry and social praxis. Thus, social crisis preaching also calls for a method of ministry and stratagem for the church's involvement in social action.

African Americans have a story that was produced by social crisis. Social crisis preaching is an effective medium for proclaiming the African American story. When theologically understood as God's call to Christian freedom and prophetically proclaimed as God's mandate for humanization, the African American story has salvific power for liberating not only the black community but this nation from oppressive practices and injustices that tend to destroy life. The African American story shapes the character of ministry in the black church. The recovery of the African American story is crucial to the goal of social ministry in the black church, which is to inspire a liberating praxis that keeps alive communal hopes and spiritual aspirations for a transformed humanity and a new social order. For me, the theological praxis of the black Christian story is consistent with the values of the kingdom of God, and therefore should serve as the basis for understanding the nature of the black

---

[1]Kelly Miller Smith, Sr., *Social Crisis Preaching* (Macon, GA: Mercer Press, 1984) 10.

church's social ministry. Black churches that desire to contribute to the development of a new social order must take seriously the challenge of social ministry: the humanizing of social structures that otherwise keep social victims in an endless cycle of social crisis.

The research and writing of this book were done in conjunction with my appointment and work as the director of the Kelly Miller Smith Institute on African American Church Studies at Vanderbilt Divinity School. The idea to inaugurate the KMSI at Vanderbilt came from Peter Paris, now the Elmer G. Homrighausen Professor of Social Ethics at Princeton Theological Seminary and Walter Harrelson, Distinguished Professor of Hebrew Bible at Vanderbilt Divinity School. Paris worked closely with Kelly Miller Smith, Sr., during the time they served on the Vanderbilt Divinity School faculty. He has been most helpful in shaping the vision of the Institute, and I am indebted to him for his lasting influence on the work of the KMSI.

To Jack Forstman, Dean of the Vanderbilt Divinity School at that time, I am also thankful for encouraging me to pursue this book. The writing of this project proceeded under the notion that the Kelly Miller Smith Institute on African American Church Studies should be established as a research institute committed to exploring the issues of faith and ministry that are important to the growth and development of the black church. Joseph Hough, Sr., current Dean of Vanderbilt Divinity School, supports this mandate of the Institute and has encouraged me to pursue its development in the work of the Institute.

I also thank Donald Beisswenger, Lewis Baldwin, Victor Anderson, Larry George, Samuel Proctor, and Peter Hodgson for their critiques of this book. Lewis Baldwin and Donald Beisswenger serve on the faculty advisory council of the Institute and have provided much encouragement, advice, and support of my work.

This book is the product of a series of annual conferences on the issue of black theology in the black church by the Vanderbilt Divinity School's Kelly Smith Institute, with the generous support of the Eli Lilly Endowment.

For the support from the people and staff ministers of the Pleasant Green Baptist Church of Nashville, Tennessee, I am also thankful.

A special word of thanks to Sherri Neal, administrative assistant, and Donna Allen, student assistant to the KMSI, for typing and re-typing the revision of this manuscript. My wife, Jacqueline, and children, Kara,

Elliott, Morgan, and Alexis, have endured through my preoccupation with the work of the Institute and the writing of this project. I am eternally grateful to them for their support, patience, and encouragement.

Finally, I am grateful to God for devoted parents, Wilbur T. and Sallie Harris, who nurtured my life and eight other children in a liberating faith that God will open up the way of freedom for us.

Introduction

The African American hunger for full human freedom (inner and outer liberation) is the foundation for the liberation-based praxis of the black church. The quest for full human freedom historically inspired the black church to address the oppressive conditions that perpetuate their disenfranchised and disposed conditions. While the quest for freedom informs black church praxis, there is a profound lack of consensus concerning the nature of the black church's liberation ministry. Developing ministry to address conditions of oppression in the black community is a complex matter fueled by divergent theologies, ecclesiologies, and current debates over euro-centrism vs. afro-centrism and civil rights vs. individual rights. Differing perceptions of liberation among black churches result in part from complex theological, ethical, economic, and socio-political problems and issues of cultural diversity and pluralism. Forming a theological perspective of praxis for addressing these issues presents a formidable challenge for the black church today.

Reflection upon ecclesial praxis no longer can be considered a low priority in the life of local black congregations. The deepening social problems of the African American community demand theological renewal of praxis in the social ministry of black churches. A praxis model in liberation is needed that enables the African American community to counter social oppression that undermines freedom under God effectively. Thus reflection upon ecclesial praxis is necessary to determine if the contemporary black church still embodies the vision of liberation that brought it into existence.

Black church ministry must be grounded in and guided by its theological heritage. The theological roots of ministry in the black church tradition connect praxis with the struggle for human wholeness and freedom. The following statement by Gayraud Wilmore identifies the issue of ministry in black churches:

> How can the black churches use the history, culture, and experience of
> their historic struggle for freedom, to enhance the proclamation of the

gospel of Jesus Christ and the manifestation of his power to transform
not only black humanity but the whole human race?[1]

Fulfilling the responsibility of this liberating vision is the special ministry
vocation of African American Christians. What type of praxis should be
undertaken by the black church to fulfill this special vocation? This study
is an attempt to respond to that question. In the black church, an adequate
response to this question, however, requires awareness and appreciation
for the dilemma of ministry. Liberating praxis *is* the church's ministry/
vocation. Liberation praxis is confrontational, invites constructive self-
criticism, and is a source of affirmation for the church's ministry. It
heals, unites, and pushes the limits of theology and ministry.

The Dilemma of Ministry in the Black Church

The Civil Rights era looms large in the memory of black Christians as
a period that enlivened liberation consciousness in local churches. In their
recent study, *The Black Church in the African American Experience*, C.
Eric Lincoln and Lawrence H. Mamiya point out that "the Black Church
has often found itself repeating history it had already experienced, and re-
learning lessons it had long since forgotten."[2] An important lesson the
black church should remember from the Civil Rights movement is that,
while the movement served as a prophetic criticism of American society,
it demanded prophetic self-criticism and internal transformation of the
black church as well.

How did the events of the Civil Rights movement increase the effectiveness of black churches in social ministry? The training that the black
church received for direct non-violent social action and service projects
was an important achievement of the Civil Rights movement. Ecclesial
and structural weaknesses in the black churches, however, remain as a
major problem in developing competence for social ministry.

---

[1]Gayraud S. Wilmore, *Black and Presbyterian: The Heritage and the Hope*
(Philadelphia: Geneva Press, 1983) 84.

[2]C. Eric Lincoln and Lawrence H. Mamiya, *The Black Church in the African
American Experience* (Durham: Duke University Press, 1990) xii.

The black church served as a viable center of the Civil Rights movement and shared the movement's unalterable commitment to telling the truth about racial injustice in American society. The Civil Rights movement in the black church, however, also demanded structural monitoring and critical analysis of praxis for addressing the social plight of the African American community. Important to the task of ministry in the black church is an understanding of its ecclesial identity through reflection on the theological basis and social purpose of its ministry.

The dilemma of ministry faced by the contemporary African American community parallels the theological perspective of ministry and leadership emerging from the black church of the post-Martin Luther King, Jr., era. It has become increasingly difficult for the black church since the King era to provide a collective definition of its theological, economic, and socio-political situation.

During the "kairos moments"[3] of the mid-1950s to the mid-1970s, the black church's self-understanding was ripe for prophetic social action. This current period of socio-political confusion has resulted in the deterioration of communal social consciousness and collective values for determining the future of the African American community. William Julius Wilson reports in his book, *The Truly Disadvantaged*, that during the twenty-year period immediately following the Civil Rights movement the social conditions of African Americans in urban centers deteriorated at an alarming rate:

—For a decade the poverty rate failed to drop, and the unemployment rate doubled for African Americans.

—In 1984 nearly one of every two persons arrested for murder and non-negligent manslaughter was African American.

---

[3]Gayraud Wilmore describes the ministry dilemma of black churches during the period between 1955 to 1975 as a "kairos moment" full of transcendent meaning, unprecedented illumination, and urgent decision-making regarding faithfulness or faithlessness toward the divine goal of love and justice. The challenge of this "kairos moment" passed unfulfilled with a diminished commitment to revolutionary struggle in America, generally, and in the black community, particularly. See Gayraud S. Wilmore, "Black Theology and Pastoral Ministry," in *The Pastor as Theologian*, ed. Earl E. Shelp and Ronald H. Sunderland (The Pilgrim Press: New York, 1988) 44.

—Black births outside of marriage dramatically rose as well as African American families headed by women; welfare dependency among poor African Americans mushroomed.

—Young African American males dropped out of school and the labor force in record proportions.[4]

The social deterioration described by Wilson parallels the dismantling of social reforms of the Civil Rights movement. This rampant deterioration began in 1969 by the politically conservative platform of Richard Nixon and continued through the administrations of former Presidents Ronald Reagan and President George Bush.[5] This erosion of Civil Rights gains continued with the anti-affirmative action policies of the Bush administration. Vital human services under the federal entitlement programs significantly diminished through Reagan's trickle-down economic policies. "Benign neglect" at the federal level, combined with the wedding of neo-conservative politics with fundamentalist religious zeal, nearly stamped out the social progress of the Civil Rights movement. This period of "benign neglect" has had a disastrous effect on liberation activism in the African American community generally and in the black church particularly.[6] For example, the crisis of the black male prison population has become a major social problem in urban black communities across the country.

Substantial change in societal structures that perpetuate the chronic social crisis mentioned above requires in-depth social and theological analysis.[7] An in-depth social analysis connected with a theological vision of social liberation will enhance significantly the black church's efforts

---

[4]Julius Wilson, *The Truly Disadvantaged: The Inner City, the Underclass, and Public Policy* (Chicago: University of Chicago Press, 1987) ch. 2.

[5]Gayraud S. Wilmore, *Black and Presbyterian*, 84.

[6]See Gayraud Wilmore's "A Revolution Unfulfilled, But Not Invalidated," in James H. Cone, *A Black Theology of Liberation*, 20th anniversary ed. (New York: Orbis Press, 1990) 155.

[7]I argue later in this study that theological reflection and social action must be responsibly linked together to support the pragmatic development of effective social ministry. See Gayraud Wilmore's, "Black Theology and Pastoral Ministry: A Challenge to Ecumenical Renewal and Solidarity," 44.

to respond to the uncontrolled pathology and social oppression currently found in the African American community.

Although black church leaders have responded to current urban social ills with courage and imagination, the scale of the problems, the scarcity of resources, and weaknesses in the black church's structure, however, make it increasingly difficult for black church leadership to develop appropriate liberation strategies for social action ministry. These factors, in part, limit the praxis response of black churches to be that of social services to victims. Advocacy and social action ministry aimed at social change have been more difficult to structure in the ministry strategy of black churches.

Structural responses of black denominations have been limited and marginal in helping congregations plan social ministry. Lawrence N. Jones' article, "The Black Church: A New Agenda," cites several weaknesses in the black church's structure that contribute to the church's inability to provide leadership in restructuring an effective social ministry. They are:

—The black church has not developed effective centralized bureaucracies.

—Church unity is expressed primarily in annual or quadrennial meetings rather than in integrated mission.

—Black churches have not devised the means for generating financial surpluses sufficient to enable them to maintain national staffs.

—Generalized economic deprivation of the African American "underclass" and the social isolation created by the social advancement of African American "middle class" have contributed to the continued fragmentation of the black religious community.

—A high percentage of the African American clergy lacks formal theological education.

—Black church people receive limited guidance from their national judicatories on such issues as drugs, AIDS, homosexuality, social trends, sexism, family concerns, and the like.

—A male-clergy leadership style dominates the black church.

—A one-dimensional understanding of ministry and Christian education persists in the black church.[8]

This assessment by Lawrence Jones, although made a decade ago, nevertheless is accurate in highlighting unresolved problems in the structures of black denominations and local black churches. Progress is slow in revisioning the ecclesial structures vital to prophetic and theological renewal of liberation praxis in the black church. In my view, these ecclesial weaknesses and the lack of significant discourse regarding theology, praxis, and social action strategies at both denominational and congregational levels create serious problems for effective praxis. Black Christians seek the renewal of a prophetic movement that will reconstitute a comprehensive praxis that will address their need for inner and outer total liberation.

Studies by theologians, sociologists, and historians of the black church experience illustrate the critical role the black church's ministry plays in the liberation struggles of the African American community.[9] Studies on the black church's liberation tradition, however, give limited

---

[8]Lawrence N. Jones, "The Black Churches: A New Agenda," *The Christian Century* 96:14 (April 1–18, 1979): 434-38.

[9]Selected literature on the liberation tradition of the black church includes: C. Eric Lincoln, *Race Religion and the Continuing American Dilemma* (Hill and Wang: New York, 1984); C. Eric Lincoln and Lawrence H. Mamiya, *The Black Church in the African American Experience* (Durham: Duke University Press, 1990); Enoch H. Oglesby, *Ethics and Theology from the Other Side: Sounds of Moral Struggle* (New York: University Press of America, 1979); Peter J. Paris, *Social Teachings of the Black Churches* (Philadelphia: Fortress Press, 1985); Gayraud S. Wilmore, *Black Religion and Black Radicalism* (New York: Doubleday, 1973); James DeOtis Roberts, *Roots of a Black Future: Family and Church* (Philadelphia: Westminster Press, 1980); Archie Smith, Jr., *The Relational Self: Ethics and Therapy from a Black Church* Perspective (Nashville: Abingdon Press, 1982).

attention to a "method of praxis" for black churches. A method for praxis refers to ministry as action in reflection. Black churches under the constant pressure of social crisis are in vital need of an action-reflection model to increase their competence for an effective liberative ministry. Unless local black churches are equipped with praxis models for in-depth social and theological analysis, ministry ends up being a reactionary, occasional, and isolated response to social crisis without the power or the imagination for sustained liberation praxis. This praxis model is necessary if there is to be social change.

This study argues that effective social ministry requires that praxis be concurrent with theological reflection and social analysis. Responsible praxis (action in reflection) is necessary for raising new questions and developing a method of ministry for social transformation. Such action and reflection create an opportunity for developing a network of ministries that enables the black churches to realize their full potential as agents of social change.

Ecclesial identity is a primary factor in understanding the relationship between black theology, liberation praxis, and ministry tradition. This study argues that the black church's survival/liberation tradition is a vital component of the black church's praxis. Correlation of black theology, identity, and social ministry is crucial to the church's liberation praxis. A theology of ministry for black churches must draw from the survival and liberation tradition inherent in black people's historic struggle for full human freedom. Liberation praxis has an inner and outer meaning for black Christian spirituality. Outwardly, it means exercising the power to throw off the economic, political, and ideological yoke of oppression. Inwardly, liberation means freedom from the internalization of oppression to arrive at a proper sense of self and right relation with God and the world.

Given the critical and urgent issues that confront the contemporary black church, this study deals with issues surrounding the topic "Ministry for Social Crisis: Theology and Praxis in the Black Church Tradition." This book focuses on two areas of social ministry: theology and praxis. Regarding black church praxis, this study considers the liberation tradition of black churches. Regarding the theological meaning of ministry, this study's interest is in the Christian tradition, ecclesial life, theology, and liberative praxis that could shape social ministry for black churches.

Chapter 1

Ministry in the Black Church: An Historical Overview

In this chapter, I inquire into the historical foundation of praxis in the black church. Such an inquiry requires an analysis of the inter-relationship between survival and liberation, and the theology emerging out of the social and cultural expressions of black Christianity. Analysis of the relationships between black liberation theology, sociology, and praxis is important in order to understand the historical development of ministry in the black church.[1] A sociological understanding of the black church's mission and its theological vision of humanity is inherent in the task of liberation.[2] The primary question addressed in this chapter is: How has ministry manifested itself in outer and inner forms of liberation in the black church? What follows is a brief analysis of the sociological,

---

[1]The observation has been made by Charles Shellby Rooks that "all the serious studies of African American churches up to 1959 had been done either by sociologists or historians: W. E. B. DuBois in 1903 (a sociologist); Carter G. Woodson in 1921 (a historian); Benjamin E. Mays in 1933 (a sociologist of religion); and Ruby L. Johnston in 1954 and 1957 (a sociologist)." Rooks sees a need for defining the ministry of the black church theologically as well as sociologically. See *Revolution in Zion: Reshaping African American Ministry* (New York: The Pilgrim Press, 1990) 32.

An acceptable definition of the nature and purpose of the black church and its ministry requires both an understanding of the sociology of church and its theological tradition. C. Eric Lincoln and Lawrence H. Mamiya, *The Black Church in the African American Experience* (Durham: Duke University Press, 1990), is the most comprehensive sociological study on the black church to date. James Cone has provided the most comprehensive theological treatment of the black church. See James H. Cone, *For My People: Black Theology and the Black Church* (New York: Orbis Books, 1984).

[2]James D. Anderson and Ezra Earl Jones, *The Management of Ministry: Leadership, Purpose, Structure, Community* (New York: Harper & Row, 1978) 94.

historical, and theological factors that have shaped the vision of liberation in the black church tradition.

Liberating Praxis: Origins in the Black Church

Critical reflection in the black church's past can be revelatory for informing present ministry action. H. Richard Niebuhr has pointed out that "our past is our present in our conscious and unconscious memory. To understand such a present past is to understand one's self and through understanding, to reconstruct."[3] Reconstruction of praxis is a formidable task for contemporary black churches that seek to achieve inner and outer transformation for social victims. The liberative praxis employed by the ancestors of the black church offers enlightenment for contemporary black Christians who seek to have their social praxis informed by the black Christian tradition.

Archie Smith's use of Olin Moyd and J. DeOtis Robert's historical sketch of the development of the black church is instructive in understanding the origin and character of liberative praxis in the black church.[4] Five historical periods identified by Smith beyond the pre-Civil War period are: (1) the Formative period, from the Civil War through Reconstruction; (2) the Maturation period, from Reconstruction to the beginning of the Great Migration; (3) the Expansion-Renaissance period, from the Great Migration to the beginning of World War II; (4) the Passive Protest period, from World War II to 1955; and (5) the Radical Reassertion period, from 1955 to the present.[5] The themes of survival and liberation are evident throughout the stages of the black church's development. These themes highlight the struggle of black people for inner and outer human and social transformation.

---

[3]H. Richard Niebuhr, *The Meaning of Revelation* (New York: Harper & Row, 1975) 117.

[4]The Lincoln and Mamiya study also gives an excellent historical overview of black church and politics and will be used in this section of the study to elucidate the development of the black church's social ministry. See *The Black Church in the African American Experience*, 199-212.

[5]Archie Smith, Jr., *The Relational Self: Ethics and Therapy from a Black Church Perspective* (Nashville: Abingdon Press, 1982) 22.

In what Lawrence Levine calls "the sacred world" of slaves, praxis in freedom was born.[6] The "sacred world" of which Levine speaks is "the one connected reality" in which slaves found status, harmony, value, order, and support for their humanity. In their struggle, slaves were able to fuse the precedents of the past, the conditions of the present, and the hope of the future into "one connected reality."[7]

As Albert J. Raboteau's *Slave Religion* and John Blassingame's *The Slave Community and Slave Testimony* show, black religion in North America was the product of an indigenous hope for liberation, dignity, freedom, human welfare, and wholeness. Black religion served as a counterforce to the harsh images and influences of slavery. Efforts to shackle and subjugate the mind of slaves to accept social bondage as a permanent way of life failed, as the reflective character of black religious consciousness was in constant tension with non-freedom.

The spiritual entity that led to the emergence of liberation praxis in black religious communities was the dialectical tension that existed between the Western christianization of slaves and the African religious sensibility that slaves brought with them from Africa.[8] C. Eric Lincoln explains that this dialectical tension gave the slaves two choices:

> They could resign themselves to their fate without struggle, or they could make a conscious effort at the re-determination of their destiny and the identity within the context of their developing body of Western experience.[9]

Lincoln goes on to say: "They [slaves] did both, and in the process they became a distinctive subculture, rooted in the African heritage, and developed in the black experience in America."[10]

---

[6]Gayraud S. Wilmore, *Black Religion and Black Radicalism: An Interpretation of the Religious History of Afro-American People,* 2d ed. (Orbis Books: New York, 1984) 220.

[7]Lawrence W. Levine, *Black Culture and Black Consciousness: Afro American Folk Thought from Slavery to Freedom* (New York: Oxford University Press, 1977) 51.

[8]W. E. B. DuBois, *The Souls of Black Folk,* in *Three Negro Classics* (New York: Avon Books, 1965) 214-15.

[9]C. Eric Lincoln, *Race, Religion and the Continuing American Dilemma* (New York: Hill & Wang, 1984) 62.

[10]Ibid., 63.

In creating a synthesis between their African religious heritage and the distortions of Western interpretations of Christian faith, slaves sought to achieve inner and outer liberation. As the first expression of this liberative praxis in freedom, slaves formed the plantation's "invisible church," later transformed into the independent black church freedom movement that sought to transcend spiritually, theologically, and ideal-istically the legacy of psychological slavery and the circumstances of social enslavement that denied human freedom under God.[11]

Black people's refusal to be humiliated and to be the uncritical recipients of a religion defined and controlled by white intermediaries and interpreters fueled slave uprisings, insurrection movements, and independent freedom movement of the black church. These movements were survival and liberation responses to the internal and external desire for freedom.[12]

The fact that the inhumanity of slavery was a mighty evil visited upon the inner life and social existence of black people is well documented. Scholars like Lawrence Levine, Na'im Akbar, Archie Smith, Jr., Eugene Genovese, and John Blassingame have shown how racial oppression imprisoned the aspirations, identity, mind, motivation, perception, and identity of blacks in a maze of anti-self images. Although generations removed from the actual experience of slavery, today African Americans still carry the scars of this experience both socially and mentally, Na'im Akbar argues.[13] The black church and its liberation tradition are products of a struggle against oppression and the spiritual pain and social oppression it perpetuated. The historical carry-overs of physical enslavement, psychological slavery, and racial oppression present formidable challenges to the ministry of contemporary black churches. Thus, the burden of self-affirmation remains the basis for internal and external responses in black religious praxis.

---

[11]Ibid.

[12]Archie Smith, Jr., *The Relational Self in the Black Church*, 15.

[13]Na'im Akbar, *Chains and Images of Psychological Slavery* (New Jersey: New Mind Productions, 1984) 7.

The Pre-Civil War Black Church

During the pre-Civil War period, the religious symbolism and theology inherent in the word "freedom" shaped the black church's action in reflection.[14] Depending on the time and the socio-political context, the theological and sociological implications of freedom resulted from the forces of oppression most dominant. Before emancipation, freedom meant the release from chattel bondage and the inherent right to human dignity under God.[15] This understanding of freedom was the most persistent image in black religious consciousness. Lawrence Levine states:

> The most persistent single image the slave songs contained is that of the [freedom] of the chosen people of God. The vast majority of the spirituals identify the [slave] as "de people dat is born of God, we are the people of God, we are de people of de Lord, I really do believe I'm a child of God, I'm a child ob God, wid my soul sot free, I'm born of God, I know I am. Nor is there ever any doubt that to the promised land I'm bound to go. I walk de heavenly road, Heav'n shall-a be my home, I gwine to meet my Savior, seek my Lord and I find Him, I seek my Lord and I find him, I'll hear the trumpet sound/In the morning."[16]

The "sacred world" of the pre-Civil War black church served as the underpinning of a theology that affirmed human beings, nature, and God as a unity—distinct but inseparable aspects of a sacred whole.[17] The biblical story of freedom, particularly the liberation motif in the Hebrew Bible, was the most important resource for affirming a liberated black future. An example of this is the plantation preacher's sermon that was therapeutic in supporting the inner and outer quest for freedom. This therapeutic ministry came through the spirituality of a survival religion expressed in slave songs, tales, and the plantation preaching of slave preachers in the "invisible church." This form of praxis was pastoral and

---

[14]Lincoln and Mamiya, *The Black Church in the African American Experience,* 4.
[15]Ibid., 4.
[16]Levine, *Black Culture and Consciousness,* 33.
[17]Ibid., 32.

priestly in character, providing persons with a sense of transcendence, ultimate justice, and personal worth as children of God.

Howard Thurman describes this form of praxis as the experience of his slave grandmother on the plantation. Thurman explains that when his grandmother told the story of the plantation preacher declaring that they were not slaves but children of God, "There would be a slight stiffening of the spine."[18] This "slight stiffening of the spine," in Thurman's view, was the inner affirmation of the self and the rejection of external oppression that negated the self.

Studies by Archie Smith, Jr., Gayraud S. Wilmore, and C. Eric Lincoln support the thesis that this freedom praxis embedded and engaged the black church in the black people's struggle for total liberation of body and soul.[19] As previously mentioned, the protest and militancy of the pre-Civil War black church was communal in nature, adapting its praxis to the cultivation of group spirit, identification, and solidarity against social oppression.[20] The pre-Civil War church gave hope to its members; it existed as a moral agent for social justice change. In its basic theology and style, the pre-Civil War black church committed itself to a liberation ethic characterized by social and spiritual emancipation.

Ministry in the service of freedom, communal values, and social justice form the liberative vision for praxis in the black church tradition. As Smith correctly says, the historic black church adapted its praxis response to the demoralizing effects of inner and outer racial oppression just as the black church must today do. This is its special vocation and responsibility. Smith remarks that

> The black church is an adapting institution and a source of courage and vitality for resisting dehumanizing conditions. It was the primary and only institution black people had to deepen and to strengthen their spiritual life and to nurture and to practice Christian ethical values, to reconcile and liberate themselves.[21]

---

[18]Howard Thurman, *With Head and Heart* (New York: Harcourt Brace Jovanovich, 1979) 21.

[19]Archie Smith, Jr., *The Relational Self*, 25.

[20]Ibid., 22.

[21]Ibid.

Memory of and reflection on past praxis for outer and inner transformation is crucial. Further, Smith is correct in saying that

> The essential task of the black church is to free the inner life of the human subjects from repressed fears, neurotic obsessions, and other forms of internalized oppression to enable men and women to make more realistic appraisals of themselves and of their world.[22]

The Formative Period

The achievement of civic freedom was a priority ministry during the Formative Period (from the Civil War through Reconstruction). The right to unconstrained social mobility and participation in civic freedoms was theologically understood as God's gift of "inalienable rights."[23] During this period, black church praxis gave impetus to strategies for communal survival and socio-political liberation. For the most part, the ministry of the black church during this period can be described thusly.

> Led by illiterate preachers, many of whom were recently freedmen, poverty-stricken and repressed by custom and law, this church converted thousands, stabilized family life, established insurance and burial societies, founded schools and colleges, commissioned missionaries to the far corners of the world, developed community political education and action in behalf of civil rights, and provided the social, economic, political, and cultural base of the entire black community in the United States.[24]

During this period, the liberating presence of black churches, through social outreach in the community, sparked exceptional growth in black church membership.

---

[22]Ibid., 26.

[23]Lincoln and Mamiya, *The Black Church in the African American Experience,* 4.

[24]Gayraud S. Wilmore and James H. Cone, eds., *Black Theology: A Documentary History, 1966–1979* (New York: Orbis Books, 1979) 244.

The Maturation Period

Political engagement combined with educational uplift highlights the character of ministry during the Maturation period (from Reconstruction to the beginning of the Great Migration).[25] Black churches offered their resources, membership, and facilities to lobby for political representation. The black church's political associations during this period reinforced it as the center of black social and political life. Social structures of justice that protected the disadvantaged from the abuse of unjust laws shaped the political agenda. Theologically, black churches saw themselves as supporting the politics of compassion and divine justice.

The politics of racial equality through law and education raised hope for a new social order. Gains in electoral politics provided opportunities for blacks to hold political office at various levels of government. Ministry vocation for black religious leaders was expressed politically as many of them sought and won political office.[26] During this period, the nature of ministry in black churches during this period was that of political support and education of social victims, particularly the self-help model of education and uplift introduced by Booker T. Washington at Tuskegee Institute and Nannie Burrough's Women Industrial Training School in Washington, D.C.[27] Global outreach ministries were also expressed in African mission during this period.

Before the end of the period, however, legal disenfranchisement of blacks regained ascendancy in political structures, and the resurgent cycle of white supremacy (Jim Crowism) stripped blacks of political gains in government.[28]

---

[25]E. Franklin Frazier, *The Negro Church in America* (New York: Schocken Books, 1974) 29.

[26]Wilmore, *Black and Presbyterian: The Heritage and the Hope* (Philadelphia: Geneva Press, 1983) 43.

[27]Ibid.

[28]Archie Smith, Jr., *The Relational Self*, 22.

The Expansion-Renaissance

Gayraud S. Wilmore describes the Expansion-Renaissance period as a critical historical time in the social development of the black church's ministry. Wilmore states that in no other period of American history did the masses of blacks need the church more desperately than between the turn of the century and the Great Depression. He observes:

> Blacks were more segregated and discriminated against by the time of the First World War than they were in 1850. Racism was rife in all sections of the nation. An unprecedented wave of lynchings, Ku Klux Klan and other anti-Negro hate groups, violence and dire poverty in the black community forced blacks to seek sanctuary in the North. The great migration brought millions of former agrarian tenant farmers from the rural South into northern cities. The demand on black churches for social services for people who often arrived at the railroad stations with all their earthly possessions in burlap sacks was overwhelming.[29]

According to Wilmore, the identity of the church as an agent of black solidarity and liberation collapsed under the demand for social services to the urban poor. New pressure from the increase of sects and cults sprang up in the ghetto to feed the psychological hungers as well as political and economic aspirations of the masses.[30] During this period, Wilmore argues, the institutional black church tended toward "social deradicalization"[31] of its ministry to the masses. Urban poverty pressed blacks into a survival mode, far different from the assertiveness of the

---

[29]Wilmore, *Black and Presbyterian*, 43.

[30]Ibid.

[31]Gayraud Wilmore argues that the "social deradicalization" of the black denominational churches and their subsequent passivity toward "social radicalism" during the Great Migration can be linked to an accommodating religiosity fueled by orthodox Christianity, theology, and lifestyle of the mainline white denominations. See Wilmore, *Black Religion and Black Radicalism,* 144. Peter J. Paris claims that an "ambiguous social ethic" associated with what W. E. B. DuBois called "the double-consciousness" of African Americans placed serious restraint on the black church's socio-political involvement for black liberation. Higher priority was given to socio-political acceptance by the dominant society rather than to social radicalism. See Paris, *The Social Teachings of the Black Churches* (Philadelphia: Fortress Press, 1985) 28.

Reconstruction and post-Reconstruction era. Marcus Garvey's Universal Improvement Association, Father Divine's Peace Mission, Daddy Grace's House of Prayer, and Black Pentecostalism were quasi-secular/cultic movements that, in some cases, attracted the poor masses more than the institutional black churches.[32] This period also led to the establishment of black secular organizations such as the National Association for the Advancement Colored People (NAACP) and the Urban League, which slowly took over the leadership for developing social action strategies for liberation of the masses.

The Passive Protest Period

Between the end of the World War II and 1955 (the Passive Protest period), social welfare represented the greatest need of blacks trapped in urban crisis. Several black churches established welfare assistance and human service programs in response to the urban social crisis.[33] Church resources were organized for meeting child care, education, economic, and housing needs of the urban masses. The effectiveness of these social ministries, however, was offset due to the scale of economic suffering in the black community, limited financial resources, and the proliferation of black sects and cults. Focused attention on the plight of social victims limited the scope of ministry activities, in many cases, to social services in urban crisis. Social advocacy for political change was predominantly carried on through social agencies such as the Urban League and the NAACP. The black intelligentsia represented in black churches often supported and joined the NAACP in large numbers in response to the political incompetence and conservative moralism of the churches.[34]

Religiously, many black churches responded to the pathology of the ghetto with revivalistic Christianity infused with moral enclaves of conservative mainline religion.[35] A major study done on the black church during the depression argues that the masses were becoming increasingly

---

[32]Joseph R. Washington, Jr., *Black Sects and Cults* (University Press of America, New York: 1986) 31.

[33]Wilmore, *Black Religion and Black Radicalism,* 163.

[34]Ibid., 143.

[35]Ibid., 161.

disillusioned with the church even though the black churches remained the primary institution in the black community.[36]

The Radical-Reassertion Period

The era of Martin Luther King, Jr., falls within the Radical-Reassertion period that includes four sub-periods in the historical development of ministry in the black church: (1) the Civil Rights/Integration period, from 1954 to 1965; (2) the Black Consciousness/Black Power period, from 1960 to 1972; (3) the Reformist period, from 1973 to 1977; and (4) the present period of political conservativism and response to Neo-Racism.[37] The ministry of King had great influence upon the praxis of ministry in the black church during these subperiods.

King projected a new image of Christian praxis and social consciousness on the ministry of the black church.[38] The cultural roots of the black church's religious tradition and the social injustice of racial oppression informed King's theology, and King's theology informed his praxis.[39] More than any person in black church history, King gave a new awareness of the possibilities and power inherent in black religion for inner and outer transformation. King's "praxis" inspired in persons who lived under the fear of racial hate and violence, the "courage to be." Most importantly, as a preacher-social activist, King brought critical reflection upon the traditional praxis of the black church and increased awareness in black Christians of their power to effect social change.[40] Gayraud Wilmore, a respected interpreter of King's social ministry, states that

---

[36]Arthur Huff Fauset, *Black God of the Metropolis: Negro Religious Cults of the Urban North* (New York: Octagon Books, 1970) 21.

[37]Archie Smith, Jr., *Relational Self and the Black Church*, 23.

[38]Wilmore, *Black Religion and Black Radicalism*, 174.

[39]Lewis V. Baldwin has persuasively argued in his most recent book that the cultural roots and heritage of the black church religious tradition was the basis for King's Christian perspective of ministry. "The black religious heritage led him to believe that the black church would continue to be a flexible and adapting instrument of black liberation and survival." See *There Is a Balm in Gilead: The Cultural Roots of Martin Luther King, Jr.* (Minneapolis: Fortress Press, 1991) 224.

[40]Ibid., 175.

the peculiar genius of Dr. Martin Luther King is that he was able to translate religious fervor into social action, thereby creating political leadership under the rubric of his religious ministry . . . under . . . conditions of extreme danger and liability.[41]

King's theological understanding of ministry will be examined in a later chapter in this study. Suffice it here to note that Dr. King's praxis vision was theologically grounded in an understanding that kept together outer and inner transformation. Thus, the sermons he preached during the Civil Rights movement were basically pragmatic and pastoral, attending to the internalized fears and social repressions that permitted an illusion of freedom, liberation, and self-determination. In the sermon "Antidotes For Fear," King shows sensitivity to the inner and outer needs of the African American community.

Courage is self-affirmation "in spite of" . . . that which tends to hinder the self from affirming itself. It is self-affirmation in spite of death and nonbeing, and he [sic] who is courageous takes the fear of death into his self-affirmation and acts upon it.[42]

King's model of social ministry merits the theological reflection of black churches as black Christians seek to develop praxis strategies for the performance of liberation ministry.

Conclusion

This brief analysis of the historical development of the black church suggests that in response to inner and outer oppression, a complex praxis tradition of survival and liberation shaped the praxis of the black church. The survival tradition arose primarily among the slaves. It continued through the struggles of the disinherited and dispossessed as an antidote to their social suffering.

Survival and liberation are the most dominant characteristics and regulative principles of ministry in the black church tradition. The

---

[41]Ibid., 174.

[42]Martin Luther King, Jr. *A Testament of Hope: The Essential Writings of Martin Luther King, Jr.*, ed. James M. Washington (San Francisco: Harper & Row, 1986) 512.

oppressed community's basic obsession with survival and liberation demanded that the church show black people how to make it, how to hold body and soul together, how to engage in an unceasing interior struggle to preserve physical existence, mental sanity, and self-respect.[43] In the following section I will make clear some of the implications the liberation and survival tradition suggest for theological reflection on the praxis of the black church.

Liberation and Survival Tradition: Implication for Ministry

The ministry of the black church is dedicated to the survival and liberation of black people. Without the black church, black people could not have survived the harsh circumstances of oppression. The special task of black Christians today is to embody the black church's liberation tradition in their ministry. The black church's history of liberation ministry began with the determination to survive. The black church must continue in this model of praxis if it is to offer alternative strategies for liberation and self-determination.

The black church's ministry means more than survival; its ministry is dedicated to liberation. Liberation goes beyond survival strategies to strategies for social elevation, organized social action, and moral resistance.[44] The liberation and survival models of ministry have existed side by side throughout the black church's history. To render itself useful for black liberation, the black church must identify and use the resources of the liberation/survival traditions to advance its mission of inner and outer transformation.

The themes of survival and liberation reinforced the corporate and pragmatic function of the black church. The black church's cultural vocation, as God's agency for ordering and improving both the inner and outer dimensions of black existence, remains the foundation of the church's ministry.[45] The black church's cultural vocation for a liberative praxis must be comprehensive. Both the pragmatic spirituality of the

---

[43]Wilmore, *Black and Presbyterian,* 46.
[44]Ibid., 224.
[45]Ibid, 48.

black religious experience and the social contradictions of the black existence are inseparable and must be kept together in the ministry of the church. The following scheme illustrates the interrelationship of survival and liberation in the ministry tradition.

The Black Church's Ministry Tradition	
Survival Tradition	**Liberation Tradition**
Self-Affirmation A God-Given Humanity	Self-Help and Self-Reliance
Interior Freedom	Interior/External Freedom
Social Denial	Social Liberty
Social Acceptance	Social Conflict
Moral Tolerance	Moral Resistance

This conceptual scheme describes the interrelational elements of the survival and liberation traditions that shape the praxis of the black church. The *telos* (end-goal) of both the survival and liberation traditions is freedom, that is, changing oppressive conditions that deny human wholeness. In the pursuit of freedom, the black church's praxis is centered in the concern of "how to make and keep life human."[46]

Theologically, the black church's liberation and survival tradition embraces the gospel as a mandate for humanization. Viewed from this perspective, the gospel focuses on full human development (inner and

---

[46]Wilmore, *Black Religion and Black Radicalism*, 225.

outer liberation) under the freedom of God. This is what black liberation theologians mean by the statement that liberation of black people from oppression is commensurate with God's self-disclosure in Jesus Christ. As explained by Archie Smith, Jr., praxis in the black church tradition might be understood as social response to the pattern of God's justice and emancipating activity in the oppressed community.[47] This understanding of ministry calls for involvement of the church in the survival and liberation of oppressed social victims.

Praxis in the contemporary black church requires that responsible use be made of the historical and theological resources in the ecclesial community's liberation/survival tradition. Thus, there are at least four emphases in the survivalist/liberationist tradition that can be used to inform the contemporary black church's understanding of liberation ministry.[48]

1. Social Justice as the Will of God

Black people know what oppression means. They also know that much of their oppression is perpetuated by religious perspectives that exalt God at the expense of freedom and justice. As J. DeOtis Roberts notes:

> Much oppression is sponsored in the name of God. . . . Religious intolerance is a root cause of much suffering today. It is not sufficient, therefore, to confess faith in God. God must also be understood as having an exalted character and a holy purpose for all creation, including [justice in] human life.[49]

In the history of the black church, the moral conviction persists that God demands social justice and cares for the poor and needy. The survivalist perspective and liberationist vision of black religious experience hold firm to this moral conviction that the caring nature of God connects with the hopes and aspirations of the oppressed in their quest

---

[47]Archie Smith, Jr., *The Relational Self,* 24.

[48]Wilmore, *Black and Presbyterian,* 96.

[49]J. DeOtis Roberts, *Black Theology in Dialogue* (Philadelphia: Westminster Press, 1987) 19.

for social justice.[50] The black church's commitment to social justice goes back to the independent black church movement, the black church's support of abolitionism, and the liberationist/survivalist strategies of the Underground Railroad.[51] The concept of God's ultimate justice and care for the poor and oppressed is the primary emphasis of praxis in the black church.

The moral conviction that God demands social justice and cares for the poor and oppressed is the basic hermeneutics of ministry in the black church religious tradition. As Howard Thurman points out in his book, *Jesus and the Disinherited*, this basic hermeneutics of ministry refers to the relationship of the religion of Jesus to the social needs of the oppressed. Howard Thurman comments:

> What does the gospel have to say to persons who have their backs against the wall? . . . The basic fact is that Christianity as it was born in the mind of [Jesus] appears as a technique of survival for the oppressed. Jesus announced the good news that fear, hypocrisy, and hatred, the three hounds of hell that track the trail of the disinherited, have no dominion over them.[52]

The moral conviction that God demands social justice and cares about what happens to the oppressed is an integral part of liberative praxis of the black church.

2. Communal Identity—A Sense of Community

In their quest for total liberation, African Americans have placed emphasis on personal and group freedom. As shown in the discussion of the plantation "invisible church," the independent black church movement and the black cultic sects of Northern urban centers are unique expressions of black people's quest for collective self-consciousness through religious communities. A communal ethos emerged in the black

---

[50]Enoch H. Oglesby, *Ethics and Theology from the Other Side: Sound of Moral Struggle* (New York: University Press of America, 1979) 19.

[51]Wilmore, *Black and Presbyterian*, 96.

[52]Howard Thurman, *Jesus and the Disinherited* (Richmond: Friends United Press, 1949) 29.

community where the art of survival was perfected and liberation strategies were tested. Collective consciousness and communal values were nurtured in the black church and the black family. Through the black church and the black family, the black community has not only survived, but it has also developed a unique culture of self-determination and liberation. Lawrence W. Levine remarks:

> Upon the hard rock of racial, social, and economic exploitation and injustice black Americans forged and nurtured a culture: they formed and maintained kinship networks, made love, raised and socialized children, built a religion, and created a rich expressive culture in which they articulated their feelings and hopes and dreams.[53]

The black church as "the cultural womb" of the black community provided hope, assurance, and a sense of group identification. It served as a source of power and self-definition alternative to the dehumanizing anti-self images in the dominate society. The black community itself is a resource for the contemporary ministry of the black church. Without a commitment to liberative praxis, social solidarity, communal consciousness, collective self-definition, and uplift, the black church is without the anchor that connects it with its liberation history.

3. Black Church Worship

Worship in the black church tradition is a primary resource for understanding the relationship between the church's liberative praxis and self-affirmation. The spiritual resources of the black church worship experience enabled African Americans to survive the powers of social oppression that have sought to destroy them. In prayers, sermons, songs, and story, African Americans unify the secular and sacred into a unique expression of self-affirmation and worth. The music, prayers, songs, sermons, and story of black Christians have served as primary sources for action in reflection toward spiritual and social transformation.

Although denied social adjustment and external freedoms, through the artistry and creative style of black worship, African Americans have been able to transcend the narrow confines of an oppressive society in

---

[53]Levine, *Black Culture and Black Consciousness*, xi.

which they were forced to live. Black religious worship provides African Americans with meaningful forms of personal integration and social solidarity. In the worship experience, African Americans found a method to be in continual dialogue with the secular realities of the community and at the same time to affirm a deeper self-worth as children of God. The character of black worship is infused with a sense of change, transcendence, ultimate justice, and personal worth. Contemporary black churches are rediscovering the communal power that ancestors of black faith expressed in the spiritual, "I'm so glad trouble don't last always, glory alleluia."

African Americans have used the resources of the black worship experience as a distinct spiritual entity for defining both their faith and involvement in social reform. In the Civil Rights rallies of the 1960s, the Southern Christian Leadership Conference used the style of black worship as the principle mode for encouraging involvement of grass- roots church leaders and laity in social action. A rediscovery of the power inherent in black worship and its relationship to social action is important for effective and responsible social praxis in the contemporary black church.

4. Biblical Images of Freedom

The symbols and images of freedom as pictured in the language of the Bible inform the moral and social response of historic black churches. Blacks have used the truth revealed in the Bible to authenticate their experience of suffering and to make sense of that experience.[54] The black church has used the Bible to discern the meaning of black existence and freedom under God. Blacks employed a "liberating and survival" hermeneutics to uncover the rich meaning of freedom in the Bible.

Ministry in the black church is guided by what Peter J. Paris calls "the black Christian tradition," a biblically based, anthropological principle of "human equality under the parentage of God."[55] The liberating hermeneutics Paris associates with "the black Christian tradition" lies in the connection he makes between blacks acting as "agents of social

---

[54]Wilmore, *Black Religion and Black Radicalism*, 1.
[55]Peter J. Paris, *Social Teachings of the Black Churches*, 10.

change" and not as "mere victims of social oppression."[56] The biblical images of freedom, particularly the Old Testament account of Egyptian bondage and liberation, are primary texts black churches have used to constitute black moral life and ethical response to social injustice.[57] Black slaves, for example, perceived the God of the Bible as a God of freedom who gives supreme importance to the norm of justice for all people in human society.

The liberating hermeneutics of black Christians was based on their own interpretations of the Hebrew Bible and Christian scriptures.[58] This is why in the black liturgical style certain scriptures are repeated themes in black people's prayers, songs, and sermons (Exod 3:7,8; Luke 4:18; Amos 5:24; Dan 3). These passages include the New Testament accounts of the resurrection of Jesus. The biblical message of human salvation that emphasized the right of freedom for all persons is the vision on which ministry in the black church is historically and theologically based. A reexamination of biblical images of freedom is important in the contemporary black church's quest for social empowerment and transformation.

In conclusion, this historical overview indicates that these four basic aspects of the liberation and survival tradition inform the praxis of the black church. Historically, black religious leaders and black Christians shared a vision of liberation and have seen themselves as agents of social change in spite of extreme social limitations.

The following chapter explores the theological criteria necessary to develop a social ministry in the black church.

---

[56]Ibid., 34.

[57]Levine, *Black Culture and Black Consciousness*, 33.

[58]Lincoln and Mamiya, *The Black Church in the African American Experience*, 202.

Chapter 2

Criteria for
Social Ministry: Black
Church Perspective

In his book *Social Crisis Preaching*, Kelly Miller Smith, Sr., comments:

> Perhaps more than anyone else of the present era, Martin Luther King, Jr., called this generation to creative, effective, and persistent social ministry. This ministry must be carried out through the proclamation of the uncompromising Word of a caring God and through the concrete courageous action required by the Word.[1]

In this statement, Smith calls attention to the social ministry that Martin Luther King, Jr., inspired in the black church and community during the Civil Rights era. Many social action efforts today seek renewal of the 1960s battle for civil rights in the 1990s. Each January, black churches become nostalgic over the King era, celebrating his birthday, hearing speeches, and having symbolic marches in hopes of keeping the dream of King's alive. But as Smith correctly says, "No mere recital of a few of King's accomplishments can exhaust the meaning of King"—the essence of his prophetic hope and praxis "cannot be accomplished simply by [celebration of] his birthday."[2]

The celebration of the life and work Martin Luther King, Jr., by contemporary black churches should motivate reflection on the praxis inspired by the liberating activities of the King era. The ministry of Martin Luther King, Jr., may be viewed as an attempt to link the spirituality

---

[1]Kelly Miller Smith, Sr., *Social Crisis Preaching* (Macon, GA: Mercer University Press, 1984) 76.

[2]Ibid., 76.

of the black church and liberating praxis in the gospel.[3] The goal of King's praxis was to destroy the moral evil of racial oppression and segregation that demoralized the image of God in people and blocked the possibility of genuine community.

The heightened enthusiasm and social promises of the King era did not produce comprehensive social changes in the infrastructure of the black community as expected. Because the movement was situated in Christian moral discourse, it rhetorically reinforced the hope in the black church and larger community that moral/political transformation of both the black community and enemies to black freedom would take place.[4]

The departure from what was termed "interposition and nullification" was seen as a sign of hope for inner and outer transformation of black existence. The strategies applied through non-violent direct action for voting rights, and ending public segregation accomplished much. The liberation brought by the social activism of that period, however, painfully exposed the fact that the black masses were caught up in new forms of racism and societal oppression, systemic poverty, and political powerlessness.

Urban demographics and poverty trends show that current political activity in urban areas has been a crude battle for resources between oppressed blacks and poor whites. The black community is considered hopelessly lost in a collection of pathologies—drug addition, illegitimacy, and crime.[5] A paralysis of fear locks the "underclass" in the poverty of inner cities and runs frightened middle-class blacks to suburban life with only marginal contact through membership in remaining black churches. As an "agency of hope," the black church remains to face the formidable challenge of being a liberating presence in the black community.

It has become increasingly obvious to the black community that access to non-segregated public facilities and leadership in electoral politics has had marginal impact on economic sources of black suffering as well as the need for organizing the community's resources for liberation. Black churches are discovering that some of the greatest needs are

---

[3]Archie Smith, Jr., *The Relational Self: Ethics and Therapy from a Black Church Perspective* (Nashville: Abingdon Press, 1982) 76.

[4]E. J. Dionne, Jr., *Why American People Hate Politics* (New York: Simon & Schuster, 1991) 338.

[5]Ibid., 338.

institutional, structural, systemic, and deeply rooted in the culture. These complex social crises require new ministry strategies and a refinement of the black church's theology and praxis.

New strategies undergirded by critical theological reflection on liberative praxis are necessary, in the ministry of black churches, to reverse the cycle of decline, violence, misery, and despair in the black community. Because existential experiences keep the pressure on black churches to respond to continuous social crisis, little time and priority are given to theological reflection on the foundation of praxis in the black church.

A strength of King's ministry was its reflective character in the middle of social crisis. King's ministry was one of action in reflection —praxis. King's *Strength to Love, Strides Toward Freedom, Why We Can't Wait*, and *Trumpet of Consciousness* were reflective discourses that gave theological and social analysis to the problems of poverty, racism, classism, and militarism. Although under the constant indictment of social crisis, ministry in the black church must be rooted in reflection, that is, reflection on its liberating activities.

This chapter outlines criteria for theological reflection on a liberating praxis in the black church. The criteria crucial for a liberative ministry in the black church are: (1) the black Christian tradition, (2) the biblical story, (3) community as a metaphor for social ministry, (4) critical self-awareness: the black church experience, (5) black liberation theology and the black church, and (6) ecclesial life as agent of human liberation.

The Black Christian Tradition

Whenever and wherever we talk of the subject of ministry in the black church, the matter of "relational wholeness" is bound up with practical concerns for inner and outer liberation. Peter J. Paris has shown in his *Social Teaching of Black Churches* how relational wholeness or rela-tionality has been normative for praxis in black churches through what he calls "the black Christian tradition."[6] According to Paris, the principle of divine and human interrelatedness (God, the world, and all races)

---

[6]Peter J. Paris, *Social Teachings of the Black Churches* (Philadelphia: Fortress Press, 1985) 10.

shapes the black church's understanding of Christian praxis. Paris argues that a biblical-based anthropology, "the parenthood of God and the kinship of all people," is normative, in black Christian praxis, for integrating religion, politics and morality, and inner and outer transformation.

Keeping together the relational dimensions of inner and outer liberation in ministry to oppressed communities is a significant problem for black church praxis. Here, the concern includes the psychological and sociological accounts of human bondage that are relevant to the relational wholeness of black people. The problem is to bring together into a significant unity knowing, doing, and being. This problem implies that reflection, social action, and selfhood interrelate and must be an active part of what it means to black and Christian in the world. When there is discontinuity between these elements (knowing, doing, being) in the church's ministry, resources for engaging the pressing matters of human oppression are not sufficiently tapped.

Resources for liberating ministry extend beyond therapeutic considerations or individualized solutions to the human brokenness of oppressed communities. As Paris explains, the concept of relational wholeness (human interrelatedness) takes seriously the communal and communitarian values espoused in the black Christian tradition.[7] Linda James Myers refers to this concept of human kinship and interrelatedness as the Afrocentric world view of human community. Myers rightly observes that the black Christian tradition is couched in a holistic world view—"I am because we are and because we are, therefore, I am."[8]

This Afrocentric world view supports Archie Smith's idea of relationality as a paradigm for ministry in the black church. Smith argues in his book *The Relational Self: Ethics and Therapy from a Black Church Perspective*, that "both outer and inner transformation are necessarily part of the same process of genuine social transformation."[9] Smith's thesis is based on the central importance of relationality in the black religious experience. Relationality, for Smith, means that human relationships are constituted in historical context and reconstituted in relationship with others and God.

---

[7] Ibid., 25.

[8] Linda James Myers, *Understanding an Afrocentric World View: Introduction to an Optimal Psychology* (Dubuque: Kendall and Hunt Publishers, 1988) 19.

[9] Archie Smith, Jr., *The Relational Self*, 14.

As defined by the black Christian tradition, the Afrocentric perspective of relational wholeness or human oneness represents an image of human community for reflecting on the biblical story of freedom under God and understanding the biographies of members of oppressed communities. Smith contends that "when the biographies of [oppressed] men and women are told and taken seriously, we can better discern the connections between their stories, [the biblical story] and the social history in which they participate, and help create and can help transform."[10]

Relationality as a paradigm for ministry in the black church entails a praxis model that takes seriously the biblical story of liberation and the black Christian story of struggle for freedom. This model of praxis requires a thorough examination of one's own story or situation in life as the basis for meaningful participation in liberation ministry. A relational understanding of ministry allows for the effective addressing of complex issues of black survival and liberation and the double burden of inner and outer oppression.

A relational paradigm for the praxis of liberation ministry also is alert to how theology, the church and world, and the socio-economic and political interests of the black community hang together. The critical nature of social problems in oppressed communities requires a form of liberation that is both structural and personal. In other words, the current situation in the black community calls for humanization of social structures. Thus, this form of liberation is the mandate of the gospel, as liberation theologies rightly declare.

Praxis as a liberation response to social oppression must be devoted to the biblical story of "leading persons out" of internalized oppression to human and social transformation. In gospel terms, it is "the power of God unto salvation" (Rom 1:15). I agree with the view of Paulo Freire in his *Pedagogy of the Oppressed*, that the struggle for liberation must keep together action and reflection, inner and outer transformation. If black churches are to "lead out" persons from internalized oppression "knowing, doing, and self-understanding" are necessary for effective liberation praxis.

---

[10]Ibid., 28.

It is becoming increasingly difficult for black Christians to find common ground for achieving and sustaining a form of liberation that addresses both inner human and outer social transformation. Divisions among black church leaders regarding (1) a theology of social change and political action, (2) evangelism and social action, (3) the relationship of black theology and the black church, (4) personal salvation and liberation, and (5) the role of black women within the church with shared leadership, are some examples that indicate that black Christians have not found a "single garment of destiny" Martin Luther King, Jr., preached. In the midst of these divisions, black Christians in local churches are left in a web of theological confusion not understanding how private troubles and public policy issues intersect with the global concerns of liberation. Closely related, this problem signals the need to push theological and biblical reflection to the center of ministry. Theological and biblical reflections on the black Christian tradition provides a foundation for the black church to examine the contemporary options and challenges of "action in reflection (praxis)."

The Biblical Story

The appeal of the biblical story upon the African American religious sensibility is that the Bible was written almost totally within a context of oppression in which images of community and noncommunity had revolutionary implications for black people's freedom.[11] The experience of oppression led the black church to an alternate view of the meaning and message of the Bible. The biblical message as originally introduced to blacks was filtered through the socio-political interests of their oppressors. But black people re-authenticated the biblical message to their need for liberation. African American biblical scholars have recently argued persuasively that the interpretative praxis employed by blacks to dismember the distortion of biblical texts had much to do with their social location and the need, as Howard Thurman noted, to validate and "stake a claim for the self" in the middle of oppression.[12]

---

[11]Cain Hope Felder, *Troubling Biblical Waters: Race, Class and Family* (New York: Orbis Books, 1989) 14.

[12]Felder, *Stony the Road We Trod* (Philadelphia: Fortress Press, 1991) 20.

In a provocative essay, "A Text for Outsiders: The Bible in African American Experience," James Evans argues that the invisibility and vulnerability of blacks in Puritan America were largely the result of flawed interpretations of the Bible.[13] Evans observes that,

> African American Christians have seen and understood the Bible as a whole text, at the center of which is the Exodus myth, the cornerstone of the Hebrew model of interpretation. They have exercised a theological imagination which, like a prism, first focuses and then refracts the biblical text. African American Christians have generally refused to dismember the biblical text without first remembering the biblical story.[14]

Evans explains further,

> Virtually every intellectual activity of African Americans was related to their condition of oppression and their desire for freedom. Thus, the hermeneutical perspective which they brought to the Bible was inseparable from their determination to live as full human beings in the presence of God.[15]

In other words, black Christians saw their story of oppression mirrored in the biblical story of liberation. The Hebrew people's liberation from non-community (slavery) and search for community (the promised land of Canaan) were symbolic for African Americans' journey to the land of freedom in America. The God of the Bible is a free God who is on the side of those seeking community and freedom. Black biblical scholars are calling for a rereading of the Bible in light of the black religious experience. This rereading of biblical texts yields new insight for the praxis of justice and love in the ministry of the church.

According to Paris, the black Christian tradition employs a distinctive hermeneutics that joins biblical assumptions about humanity with the

---

[13]James H. Evans, "A Text For Outsiders: The Bible in African American Experience," unpublished speech, delivered at the American Academy of Religion, Narrative Interpretation and Theology Group, Anaheim, California, 1989.

[14]Ibid., 9.

[15]Ibid., 19.

struggle against racial oppression.[16] In the Bible, blacks found a perspective on humanity that affirmed a non-racist appropriation of the Christian faith, that is, the universal parenthood of God and a universal kinship of humankind. The discovery of the biblical concept of human interrelatedness under the parenthood of God served as the theological ground for the black church's praxis and provided means of evaluating the authority of the Bible itself. Paris observes that "black churches have never hesitated to disavow any interpretation of scripture that legitimate any form of racial oppression."[17] Paris further notes that "one can conclude that there have been no sacred scriptures for blacks apart from the hermeneutical principle immortalized in the black Christian tradition."[18] In other words, the biblical story, for African Americans, is one of freedom.

The Black Christian Story

Story, as defined in this discussion is a metaphor for the expression of the biblical story as seen through the lenses of the black Christian story or tradition. Reflection on the biblical story and the black Christian story is the basis for bringing together action and reflection in the ministry of the black church. In terms of the black Christian story, the reference is made to the religious tradition of African Americans as embodied in the life and ministries of the black church. Reflection among congregants in the black church takes place in the telling of stories about oppression and liberation struggles.[19] Black persons' religious response to social oppression continues to be expressed in the context of the "sermon, song, and story" in the traditional worship and Bible study of black churches.

The black Christian story is a shared experience of survival and the quest for liberation. The shared story of "survival and liberation" suggests that praxis in the black church's ministry be a shared response to the

---

[16]Peter J. Paris, "The Bible and The Black Churches," in *The Bible and Social Reform*, ed. Ernest Sandween (Philadelphia: Fortress, 1982) 134.

[17]Ibid., 135.

[18]Ibid., 135.

[19]James H. Cone, *God of the Oppressed* (New York: Seabury Press, 1975) 7. As noted by Cone, African American religious response to oppression has been in the form of "sermon, song, and story."

needs of inner and outer liberation. The African American experience (black self-identity and awareness) informs black liberation praxis based on the hermeneutical meaning uncovered in the black Christian tradition.[20] The basic convictions that give shape to the hermeneutics of the black Christian story are:

(1) The God of the Bible liberates and acts historically in real events of oppression.

(2) God has been active in the history of African American's struggle for freedom.

(3) God calls and invites the oppressed to participate in the inner and outer realities of divine freedom and justice.

(4) The black church is called to embody and respond to God's freedom.

(5) God's liberating Word of freedom moves through concrete praxis.

In the quest for freedom under God, black Christians embraced a particular interpretation of the scriptures. The content of this interpretive quest is reflected in ecclesial praxis, worship, rituals, music, communal structures, and ministry. On the basis of its ecclesial praxis in freedom and interpretation of the biblical story, the black church draws its spiritual life by being in solidarity with the history of God's liberating deeds on behalf of oppressed people.

Remembering and representing the story are essential for understanding the character of black Christian's social witness and ministry. If black churches are to know and discern the nature of God's continuing actions of liberation, the story of the black Christian tradition must be

---

[20]Don E. Matthews, "Black Women's Religion, History and Praxis: Implications for a Black Liberation Praxis," *Chicago Theological Seminary Register* 78 (Spring 1988): 23-29. Matthews argues that interpretation of the black experience or story in Eurocentric philosophical frameworks, and American pragmatic thought, and denominational records do not disclose the ethics and theology of the black Christian story.

told, theologically reflected upon, and made accessible to the ongoing task of ministry.

The question that guides this reflection is: Do contemporary expressions of black ecclesial life and praxis authentically represent the biblical story as interpreted through the lenses of the black Christian tradition? This study argues that community (human interrelatedness under God) is an essential metaphor for understanding the black Christian story and nature of ministry in the black church. The experience of community and non-community shapes the black Christian story and informs a black ecclesial praxis. An essential aspect of the black Christian tradition is the quest for genuine community.

Community as a Metaphor
for Ministry in the Black Church

Western theologians, like William R. Burrows, who are in dialogue with Latin American liberation theologians and black theologians, are reevaluating the whole question of ministry under what Peter Hodgson calls "ecclesial freedom under a new paradigm." This "new paradigm" underscores liberative praxis as the essence of Jesus' earthly ministry. As William R. Burrows notes,

> The task of the church is one of helping people to realize the transcendent stakes at play in commitment to the world. The search for justice and authentic human development breaks through sacrilized, given patterns of what "must be" to help people realize that they have the possibility of shaping worlds that never have been and yet might be. Such is the intrinsic dimension of [the kingdom of God]: freedom and responsibility to enhance and to transform humanity.[21]

This "new paradigm" calls for critical engagement with the reign of God as the symbol for human existence in divine freedom, justice and community. The new paradigm also recognizes that liberation is at the

---

[21]Peter Hodgson, *Revisioning the Church: Ecclesial Life under a New Paradigm* (Philadelphia: Fortress Press, 1989) 2.

very heart of the kingdom praxis, ministry, preaching and purpose of Jesus.

The biblical symbol of the kingdom of God or "the beloved community" is deeply rooted in the black Christian story and consciousness. The reign of God, in the black Christian tradition, is a world without racism, injustice, and oppression; it is the beloved community where human relations exist under the freedom of God. The reign of God implies an active relationship between people and God wherein social and political structures are humanized toward total liberation. In the Hebrew Bible and Christian scriptures, the vision of God's reign is posed as God's own vision and intention for all people.[22] In the Hebrew Bible, the reign of God speaks of God's complete dominion over all creation (Exod 15:18; Pss 145:13; 47:3; Jer 10:7-10).[23] In the fulfillment of the reign of God, God wills love, justice, peace, freedom, wholeness, unity, joy, and an end to war and human suffering (Isa 25:6-8; 2:4; Pss 98:1-11; 146:7-10).[24]

The black Christian tradition holds firmly to the social promises of the reign of God as the church has sought to do ministry under the model of Jesus Christ. While black theologians and preachers in the black church fluctuate between a Christology from below and a Christology from above, there is a consensus that the reign of God is the central theme and message of Jesus' life. In settings where the identity of the black church and its social mission in the community are in question, often Jesus' statement recorded in Luke 4:18 is quoted and applied:

> The Spirit of the Lord is upon me, because he has anointed me to bring good news to the poor. He has sent me to proclaim release to captives and recovery of sight to the blind, to let the oppressed go free, to proclaim the year of the Lord's favor. (NRSV)

Martin Luther King, Jr., used the biblical symbol of the reign of God more effectively than any church leader of recent times. The focus of King's liberation praxis was the vision of the reign of God or the beloved

---

[22]Thomas Groome, *Christian Religious Education: Sharing Our Story and Vision* (San Francisco: Harper & Row, 1980) 35.

[23]Ibid., 36.

[24]Ibid., 38.

community as the ultimate norm and goal for civil rights, economic justice, and world peace.[25] King understood the concept of the beloved community as "the ideal new humanity" and the goal and norm of the moral life.[26] Community arises out of a context of active participation in society on behalf of the values of God's reign. In an analysis of King's conception of community, Walter Fluker notes that King understood the reign of God as rooted in the

> interrelatedness of life, the sacredness of human personality, the moral order of the universe, the personal God of love and reason who is revealed in power, and the social nature of human existence.[27]

King's praxis was grounded in the conviction of a personal God of love and power who works for universal wholeness.[28]

In conclusion, this hermeneutics of human interrelatedness determines the goal of ministry: leading people out to the reign of God in Jesus Christ. The ministry of Jesus Christ is a concrete paradigm of the divine initiative in the transformation of existence.[29] Human development in divine freedom and justice requires a vision of God's reign that supports critical self-awareness grounded in relationality and community.

Critical Self-Awareness:
The Black Church Experience

The primary source for black self-interpretation has been the black church.[30] The black church experience served as means for developing a positive black self-image and understanding of black life. The ethos of the black church (the quest for relational wholeness and freedom under

---

[25]Ibid., 137.

[26]Walter E. Fluker, *They Looked For A City: A Comparative Analysis of the Ideal of Community in the Thought of Howard Thurman and Martin Luther King, Jr.,* (New York: University Press of American, 1989) 148.

[27]Ibid., 128.

[28]Ibid., 137.

[29]William R. Burrows, *New Ministries: The Global Context,* (New York: Harper & Row Publisher, 1978) 49.

[30]Paris, "The Bible and the Black Churches," 133.

God) provide blacks with the capacity to affirm their humanity and empowers them to envision and implement alternative perceptions to the reality of oppression. An important aspect for a method of ministry in the black church is to remember the story of black Christian tradition in such a way as to develop and nurture critical self-awareness (identity). The black church experience has been one of empowerment of selfhood for involvement in the struggle for freedom.

Critical self-awareness involves what Paulo Freire calls "conscientization," that is, making oppressed people aware of their potential to determine their own destiny. Freire correctly maintains,

> No one liberates himself/herself by his or her efforts alone, neither is he or she liberated by others. . . . The correct method lies in dialogue. The conviction of the oppressed that they must fight for their liberation is not a gift bestowed by revolutionary leadership, but the result of their own conscientization.[31]

Conscientization is a process of bringing oppressed people to self-awareness of their internal and external powers to act, to reason and interpret their social context, and to be self-determining in the realization of their potential for shaping the world in freedom, justice, and love.[32] This process of conscientization is what we have referred to as the praxis of the black Christian tradition. This kind of praxis refers to action in reflection that involves the dimensions of meaning, action, and self-understanding.[33]

The meaning dimension of praxis concerns the appropriation of black Christian's understanding of God that bears self-knowledge, truth intrinsic in being.[34] As Thomas Ogletree insists, it is "disclosure of the meaning of being and our placement in it."[35] We are African Americans; therefore,

---

[31]Paulo Freire, *Pedagogy of the Oppressed*, (New York: Seabury, 1973) 54-55.

[32]Ibid., 54.

[33]Thomas W. Ogletree, "Dimension of Practical Theology: Meaning, Action, Self," in *Practical Theology: The Emerging Field in Theology, Church, and World* (Harper & Row: San Francisco, 1983) 86-101.

[34]Linda James Myers, *Understanding an Afrocentric World View*, 19.

[35]Ogletree, "Dimensions of Practical Theological: Meaning, Action, Self," in *Practical Theological: The Emerging Field In Theology, Church, and World*, ed., Don S. Browning, 86.

our blackness has its special place in the economy of God. As James Cone explains, this identity is the truth that sets us free: "Indeed it is the encounter of this truth . . . that enables us . . . to know" the essence of our being.[36] Insofar as our participation in freedom under God, our integrity as black Christians resides in our affirmation of and fidelity to the cause of our essence that is the source of our being, our life, our human dignity and worth.

The action dimension concerns the enactment of what has been disclosed in the meaning dimension of praxis. Here concepts of love, justice, and the sacredness of human personality guide ministry praxis. Praxis involves the "courage to be," to use a Tillichian phrase. This courage is the embodiment of the unity and wholeness promised to all of God's children.[37]

The self dimension of praxis leads to the inescapable question concerning the formation of the inner self (identity), that is, Who am I? What is my worth? We cannot properly define ourselves or contain our being isolated from others. The Afrocentric world view of human community holds that the definition of the self lies in community and communal relationships with others. As history of the human race reveals, isolation from community with others (the kinship of all people) distorts understanding of God, the consequences of which has resulted in brutal inhumanity and injustice against racial minorities and women in the name of God. In a holistic view of human community the kind of conscientization described here is crucial for human and social transformation.

Paulo Freire's concept of conscientization is operative at various levels of black people's struggle for freedom, especially within the many individual and corporate stories of oppression and liberation. Constant repetition of injustices, social sins, and violence against and within the black community, however, may have a dangerous narcotic effect, dulling critical conscientization and memory for understanding the importance of past liberating activity. Because African Americans are constantly assaulted by the reiteration of statistics regarding the black community's underdevelopment, continuous "action in reflection"—"knowing, doing and being"—is crucial to their liberation struggle.

---

[36] James H. Cone, *God of the Oppressed*, 38.
[37] Ibid., 86.

According to Archie Smith, Jr., liberation from oppression today requires linkage with the recollection of a forgotten past.[38] The recollection or critical memory requires what Smith calls "anamnestic solidarity," a rediscovery of the meaning of the church's task in the present time or a remembering of the past that shapes the future in a new way.[39] Anamnestic solidarity is not simply a remembrance, it calls the present to the past, and the past to the present in a way that enlivens the future. Anamnestic solidarity begins the process of critical reflection upon the black Christian story and upon present ministry in response to social contradictions under which black life exists.

The goal of community, as expressed in the black Christian tradition, is to create a world of "non-oppression" that supports the liberation of all persons for participation in God's freedom, justice, and love. Liberation implies a quality of life that honors the inherent dignity and worth of all persons. Participation in the building of community is difficult without critical self-awareness. As Smith argues, critical self-awareness undergirded by anamnestic solidarity with the past is the basis for affirming the *telos* of the church's liberation ministry, that is, the beloved community.

As previously mentioned, self-awareness and self-definition are affirmed in the context of community. The self-understanding of the black church is grounded in the conviction that God's involvement in the history of the oppressed is to create the beloved community.[40] As Walter Fluker notes, "The ultimate goal of God's creativity in persons is the realization of community."[41] Ministry involves the building of community ordered by love and justice in the relationship between persons, God, and the world.[42] Ministry is a liberating activity that forms an inclusive community of non-racism, non-sexism, and non-classism. Community in this sense supports all persons as children of God. The moral and

---

[38]Archie Smith, Jr., *The Relational Self*, 23.

[39]Ibid., 19.

[40]Walter E. Fluker illustrates this point in his comprehensive treatment of the ministry careers of Martin Luther King, Jr., and Howard Thurman. The search for community, the life long goal of Thurman and King, represents the end value for the ministry of the black church. See *They Looked for a City: A Comparative Analysis of the Ideal of Community in the Thought of Howard Thurman and Martin Luther King, Jr.*, (New York: University Press of America, 1989) xi.

[41]Ibid., 118.

[42]Ibid., 114.

political significance of the black church is derived from this concept of human interrelatedness.[43]

The black church exists in the black community as a sign of actualized community. The core quality of the black Christian tradition is its communitarian ideal of human interrelatedness grounded in divine freedom and justice. This ecclesial quality is what Tom Driver refers to as communal and communitarian existence.[44] This concept of community leads to the conclusion that relationality (communitarian existence) is a paradigm for the black church's liberation ministry. Relationality as a criteria for a method of ministry involves interaction that moves toward creativity, justice, love, liberation, and faith. These ingredients of ecclesial life in liberation praxis are further discussed in the following section.

Relationality: A Paradigm for Social Ministry

By way of summary, Archie Smith, Jr., maintains that social ministry is relational activity supported by responsible praxis.[45] Smith's concept of relationality holds together an analysis of inner and outer transformation in liberation ministries. As he puts it, "Inner and outer transformation identifies relationality and the communal self as key concepts in emancipatory struggles and liberation ministries."[46]

Relationality serves as a basis for the performance of social ministry and is compatible with the black church's understanding of community. In Smith's view, ministry as a relational activity is solidarity with persons embedded in social milieus and structures that need transformation.[47] Using George Herbert Mead's concept of "mind, self, and society" and H. R. Niebuhr's concept of "responsible self," Smith observes that a

---

[43]Peter J. Paris, *Social Teachings of the Black Churches,* 10.

[44]Thomas F. Driver, "Justice and the Servant Task of Pastoral Ministry," in *The Pastor as Servant,* Earl E. Shelp and Ronald H. Sunderland, eds. (New York: The Pilgrim Press, 1986) 53.

[45]This study refers to Archie Smith's concept of social ministry many times already and will continue to cite him throughout.

[46]Smith, *The Relational Self* , 14.

[47]Ibid., 28.

human person is a relational self, a self that comes to exist in response to other selves and in response to the radical action of God.[48]

Likewise, according to Howard Thurman, the religious experience (the direct exposure of the self to God that creates a consciousness of the presence of God within the self) transforms human energy into community-making power.[49] The self depends upon community and the community depends upon the self.[50]

In Thurman's concept of the nature of community, he determined three factors critical to the validation of the self: (1) the inner necessity to stake a claim for the self (inherent worth), (2) the demand for wholeness through fulfillment of the spiritual needs of the human spirit (worship), and (3) the need for inclusiveness that involves life in a total sense in the process of community (social and spiritual relatedness). Thurman saw the need for a healthy self image as crucial to one's participation in the ideals of community. As Walter Fluker notes in his analysis of Thurman's concept of community,

> A healthy sense of self is garnered out of a dynamic tension between the individual's self-fact and self-image. The person's self-fact is her/his inherent worth as a child of God; it is the central fact that s/he is part of the very movement of life itself. The individual's self-image is formed by relationships with others, and to a large extent, self-image determines one's destiny.[51]

A sense of self, in Thurman's view, is the ground for community with others. Thurman believed that "an individual who experiences God in personal encounter must seek to share her/his experiences of the love of God in community with others."[52] The realization of the self and the concept of community are interdependent. The committed individual is dedicated to the removal of all barriers that impede the possibility of

---

[48]Ibid., 115. Smith's concept of "the relational self" and Howard Thurman's concept of "the self" are similar.

[49]Howard Thurman, *Footprints of a Dream: The Story of the Fellowship of All People* (New York: Harper and Row, 1959) 16.

[50]Luther Smith, *Howard Thurman: The Mystic as Prophet* (New York: University Press of America, 1981) 166.

[51]Walter E. Fluker, *They Looked For A City*, 34.

[52]Ibid., 71.

becoming whole in the world. This involves creative confrontation and transformation of the cultural pattern in which people find themselves.[53] Racism, sexism, and classism are considered "contradictions of life" and inimical to the formation of identity and realizing the full potential of community.[54] Where barriers to realizing the potential and inherent worth of the self (full human development) exist, community is not possible.[55]

Relationality, in Smith's understanding, implies the social, historical, contextual, and relational character of the self, that is, "one is only human because of others, with others, for others."[56] Social relations exist in and through concrete cultural, socio-political, and economic situations wherein people are both self-determined and limited by what is given in the social order.[57] The self is socially mediated. Reflection on the social context in which the self is mediated ultimately brings one to self-identity.[58] Praxis or critical reflection on "human experience and inter-action" always involves engagement of the self, that is, the drive of the self in the search for meaning.

For Smith and Thurman, the relational self is essential for the actualization of community, that is, freedom and justice under God. When properly constituted in relationality, persons can become agents for creation of community. The concept of the relational self and image of community as a metaphor for the church's ministry requires reflection upon "What is God enabling and requiring the church to be and do?"[59] Selfhood and praxis are held together by theological reflection upon "Who are we?" In the context of black identity, this reflection necessarily must take into account what it means to be black and Christian in relation to social realities that oppress life and are barriers to community. Social ministry committed to community (kinship of all persons under the parenthood of God) and relationality (the relational and responsible self) means:

---

[53]Ibid.
[54]Luther Smith, *Howard Thurman: The Mystic as Prophet,* 97.
[55]Ibid., 105.
[56]Archie Smith, Jr., *The Relational Self,* 55.

[57]Ibid., 63.
[58]Ibid., 185.
[59]Ibid., 55.

The unity of persons around the idea that each is important enough to be respected and loved by all. It means that I want every other person to be as free and loved as I want to be. Liberation then implies a quality of life that asserts the importance and worth of persons in such a way that they are free from poverty, from control by powerful interest, from superstition, fear, hostility, or from anything that enslaves them.[60]

Black people live with the double burden of inward and outward oppression, thus making necessary the inner and outer liberation of self. If the definition of the self is distorted, persons are hindered severely in accomplishing liberation from external forms of oppression. Inner liberation of the self is critical to outward participation in the pursuit of genuine community, that is, meaningful relationality and communal identity.

Rosemary Ruether has rightly perceived the need for "resurrected self" regarding inward liberation for oppressed persons:

They [the oppressed] have been victimized by their powerlessness, their fear and their translation of these into internal appropriation of subservient and menial roles. They have internalized the negative image projected upon them by the dominant society. They cower before the masters but are also filled with a self-contempt which makes them self-destructive and fratricidal toward their fellows within the oppressed community. Typically the oppressed turn their frustration inward, destroying themselves and each other, not the master. Liberation for the oppressed thus is experienced as a veritable resurrection of the self.[61]

Christian social ministry guided by the concept of relationality and the image of community balances a theology of "politics of justice and compassion" on behalf of the oppressed with the religious experience (freedom of God in and beyond the self).[62] This process of interaction moves oppressed people toward a transformed humanity and a transformed earth.

---

[60]Ibid, 116-17.

[61]Rosemary Radford Ruether, *Liberation Theology: Human Hope Confronts Christian History and American Power* (New York: Paulist Press, 1972) 12.

[62]Walter Brueggemann, *Prophetic Imagination* (Philadelphia: Fortress Press, 1978) 18.

In conclusion, relationality as a paradigm for ministry involves theological reflection upon communitarian existence. This reflection necessarily includes critical reflection on a biblical meaning of black existence and how the theology of the church interrelates with the socioeconomic and political liberation of the black community. What it means to be black and Christian and how personal life and social structures intersect are theological concerns for praxis in the black church. The theology of the church and social mission are inseparable for reconstituting ecclesial praxis in the black church and for the empowerment and involvement of individuals in a process of liberation. What follows is a discussion of how black liberation theology manifests itself in "ecclesial freedom" and praxis in the black church.

Black Liberation Theology and the Black Church

Black theology is back on the agenda of the black church as it seeks to give a theological and holistic ministry response to current social crises. Black church leaders and theologians are looking for a revival of dialogue among them that will help close the gap between black theology and the ministry of black churches. There is increased awareness that issues of black poverty, unemployment, and political alienation are not separate matters from the theological concerns of the church. As J. DeOtis Roberts accurately says, that the dialogue between black theologians and church leaders concerning the relationship between theology and ministry is an unfinished agenda for praxis in the black church.[63]

James Harris, in his most recent book, *Pastoral Theology: A Black Church Perspective*, raises a concern that leading black theologians like James Cone, Gayraud Wilmore, and J. DeOtis Roberts have sought to resolve in their current approaches to black theology. Harris notes that black theology is foreign to black Christians.[64] Harris' claim is supported by data in the Lincoln and Mamiya study, which indicates that the

---

[63]J. DeOtis Roberts, *Black Theology in Dialogue* (Philadelphia: Westminster Press, 1987) 115.

[64]James H. Harris, *Pastoral Theology: A Black-Church Perspective* (Minneapolis: Fortress Press, 1991) 55.

objectives of black liberation theology have had relatively limited influence upon black clergy and their congregations.[65]

The problem of black theology being isolated from the Christian education programs of black churches is a complex matter and demands further investigation. In Harris' assessment of the problem, he is acutely aware that apart from each other, the black church and black theology are weak instruments for the achievement of black liberation. "Black theology has little or no practical value apart from the black church. The liberation of black people cannot be achieved without the church's engagement of black theology," Harris rightly notes.[66]

Because members of black churches have little or no knowledge of black liberation theology, they are not benefitting from its critical reflection on the nature and purpose of the black church's social mission. James H. Cone notes in his book, *For My People: Black Theology and the Black Church*, that "when black theology first emerged it had no existence a part form the black church."[67] In the writer's view, the current problem of black theology and the black church should be understood in the context of several problems related to historical praxis in the black church.

First, black Christians have always given some type of theological reflection on what it means to be a Christian in a society that denies them full freedom. They have engaged in a struggle between a political and personal theology of salvation. In this theological struggle, praxis in the black church went through the maze of Christian moralism, conservative religious ideology, and distortions of the gospel perpetuated by ecclesial racism in the white church and evangelical fundamentalism in both black and white churches. Black theology arose as a corrective to the narrowness and non-liberating understanding of God's redemptive involvement in the history of oppressed people. It was a protest against the trampled dignity of black people in an environment of racism, which was accepted and perpetuated by the white church and its theologians.

---

[65]Lincoln and Mamiya, *The Black Church in the African American Experience* (Durham: Duke University Press, 1990) 179.

[66]Ibid., 55.

[67]James H. Cone, *For My People: Black Theology and the Black Church* (New York: Orbis Books, 1984) 102.

Second, black liberation theology, which emerged as a scholarly discipline during the latter stages of the Civil Rights movement and was considered by some as a product of the movement, did not reached its original objective of informing the praxis of local black churches, due to a non-supportive infrastructure within black churches.[68] Black religious leaders within major denominations took issue with Cone's first books on black theology and discouraged the promulgation of black theology within the infrastructures of black church's Christian education programs. This objection to black theology was in response to Cone's exposure of the "hidden racism" in the Western theological tradition, a tradition that many black church leaders had accepted uncritically.

The largest body of American black Christians, the National Baptist Convention USA, Inc., under the leadership of Joseph H. Jackson, rejected black liberation theology on the grounds of its racial critique of white Christianity. Little attention was given to the potential of black theology for informing praxis in the black church. Jackson understood black theology as a theology of "race, power and politics," universally unacceptable for the salvation of the human community.[69] Black theology sought to expose the very source of the social sin in American society that kept both black and white people from the justice of the beloved community. As Gayraud Wilmore explains:

> From the beginning, the objective of black liberation theology was Christian theology reinterpreted by African Americans in an effort to understand what the gospel had to do with black suffering and struggle

---

[68]Gayraud Wilmore, "A Revolution Unfulfilled, But Not Invalidated," in James Cone, *A Black Theology of Liberation:* 20th Anniversary ed. (New York: Orbis Books, 1990) 152.

[69]Joseph H. Jackson's rejection of black liberation theology is based on his judgement that black liberation theology reduces theological truths of the Christian religion to the historic conflict between blacks and whites. Black theology, for Jackson, is too narrow to accommodate the universality of the Christian gospel of liberation. "If the Negro church accepts the point of view and the leadership of Black Theology of Liberation, then black people will become the outstanding proponents of racial segregation in the United States of America." See "An Appraisal of A Black Theology of Liberation, in the Light of the Basic Theological Position of The National Baptist Convention, U.S.A., Inc., Record of the 91st Annual Session of the National Baptist Convention, U.S.A., Inc.," in Paris, *Black Leaders In Conflict: Martin Luther King, Jr., Joseph H. Jackson, Malcolm X, Adam Clayton Powell Jr.*, (New York: Pilgrim Press, 1978) 227.

to survive genocide, to elevate themselves and their families to a higher quality of life and culture, and to free themselves and all people who needed liberation from every form of domination.[70]

Unfortunately, the praxis vision of black liberation theology suffers from the horns of the dilemma we have discussed. The reasons for this dilemma are difficult to determine fully; however, it is the writer's conviction that theological renewal of the black church's ministry is severely hindered without reflection on the praxis vision of black liberation theology.

James Harris, C. Eric Lincoln, and Lawrence Mamiya apparently locate the major responsibility for the dilemma with black theologians. They imply that the problem relates to "major formulators of black liberation theology not moving beyond their middle-class origins" and formulating black theology in language unacceptable to grass-roots black church people.[71] In the writer's view, the problem is a cultural and structural problem, having to do with discovering a form of liberation that is structural as well as personal in dealing with the need for inner and outer human transformation. Culturally, black churches are rooted and embedded in an ethical paradox between white religious values and the values of the black Christian tradition. Structurally, the political struggle against racism and other forms of oppression has been seen apart from authentic black spirituality and Christian piety, especially by conservative evangelical black churches.[72] This ethical paradox encouraged the rise of a conservative evangelicalism among black Christians that expresses little or no interest in black liberation theology. In the moral confusion of this ethical paradox regarding Christian values and praxis, many blacks during the 1970s and 1980s, as Wilmore says, "slipped back into a previous condition of cultural anonymity and bought into an unreflective, white middle class religiosity and materialistic life style."[73]

---

[70]Gayraud S. Wilmore, "Black Theology and Pastoral Ministry: Challenge to Ecumenical Renewal and Solidarity," *The Pastor as Theologian*, 47.

[71]Lincoln and Mamiya, *The Black Church in the African American Experience*, 180.

[72]Wilmore, "A Revolution Unfulfilled But Not Invalidated," in James H. Cone, *A Black Theology of Liberation*, 20th Anniversary ed., 152.

[73]Gayraud Wilmore, *Black and Presbyterian*, 84.

Today many black Christians involved in the ministry of black churches find themselves confronted again with a theological identity crisis related to the age-old problem identified by W. E. B. DuBois as African American "twoness." DuBois' prophetic insight into the African American problem of "the colorline" demands constant theological reflection. DuBois declared:

> The [African American] is . . . born with a veil, and gifted with second-sight in this American world, a world which yields him no true self-consciousness . . . It is this double consciousness, this sense of always looking at one's self through the eyes of others. . . . One even feels this twoness—an American, and [African American]; two souls, two thoughts, two bodies, whose dogged strength alone keeps it from being torn asunder.[74]

This "twoness" infuses the black religious mind with a "double consciousness" that perpetuates a theological crisis involving a constant movement of black Christians between two theological worlds, one black and the other white. As Harris notes, "While blacks labored over a double-consciousness, whites practiced a double standard."[75] Those black churches that tend to reflect the theological perspective of the Western religious values, while at the same time calling for a just social order, find it difficult to sustain an ethical praxis consistent with the black Christian tradition. Paris gives an accurate picture of this theological crisis:

> The tendency of the black churches has been to employ the thought patterns of the white churches in articulating their theological understandings. Whenever called upon to justify their social reform activities, they have no difficulty appealing to those [white] theological understandings. Black churches have seen no need for sustained theological and ethical reflection that might lead to the development of a systematic body of thought.[76]

---

[74]W. E. B. DuBois, *Souls of Black Folk,* in *Three Negro Classics* (New York: Avon Books, 1965) 214-15.

[75]James Harris, *Pastoral Theology: A Black Church Perspective,* 40.

[76]Peter J. Paris, *Social Teachings of the Black Churches,* 75.

Paris further states:

> By affirming the basic theology of the white churches, the black
> churches have failed to see the disservice they have rendered
> themselves, since the thought patterns of the white churches were not
> always commensurate with the activities of black churches, especially
> those pertaining to the embodiment of racial justice. Black churches
> have accepted wholesale [sic] the theology of the white churches and
> used it in the service of fighting racism.[77]

Black Christians, involved in the ministry task of black churches today,
continue to be trapped on the horns of this theological dilemma.

While black people need liberation from their double-consciousness,
white people need to turn from their double-standard of justice. As
Wilmore explains, the theological crisis of "double consciousness," while
being a source of the black church's weakness, can also potentially be a
source of strength for the universal goal of the gospel, that is, the coming
of the "beloved community." Wilmore states:

> The strength of African American people may well come from the gift
> of being able to combine the best of two cultures in a new life
> orientation, a new humanity, and overlaying the whole with an
> indomitable faith in God that is able to transcend the contradictions and
> delusions of all human existence.[78]

Wilmore also notes:

> The alienation and the hatred that divide and sicken the world cannot
> be overcome by secular ideologies or [denying the particularity of
> anyone religious tradition], but only by faith in God, who "has broken
> down the dividing wall . . . reconciling us to God in one body through
> the cross, thereby bring hostility to an end" (Eph 2:14,16). Thus, the
> Christian faith provides African American culture with the spiritual
> cement by which two cultures—one African and the other Euro-
> American—are reinterpreted and fused into one: a [new humanity] that
> has the power to inspire and direct [Blacks and Whites] toward the goal

[77]Ibid., 75.
[78]Wilmore, *Black and Presbyterian,* 86.

of shalom—the Hebraic idea of the welfare, the peace, the unity of the whole created order.[79]

Black liberation theology can assist black Christians in thinking theologically about their situation of oppression and how their liberation links with the redemption and transformation of the total society. This model of liberation praxis is the special responsibility to which the black church should commit its resources and talents.

What Black Christians Should Know about Black Theology

First, theology is the task of the church to discern God's work in the world. The task of every Christian in the church is to do theology, that is, to seek an understanding of how God acts in history and in the life of the human community. Theology is a human enterprise; it is developed in context of life situations and struggles. Those who do theology are making an effort to understand and declare who God is, what God demands from us as human beings, what God has done and is doing for human salvation, and in the light of that knowledge, to respond in faith and obedience to God's call for love and justice. Theology itself is not a neutral discipline. Theology reflects the contextual experience and perspective of the community out of which it arises.

Thus, black liberation theology is Christian theology, it is an effort to understand the meaning of God and God's involvement in black people's struggle for freedom and peoplehood. Black liberation theology is a reflective discourse rooted in the religious experience of black people with God.[80] The task of black liberation theology is to discover more adequate ways of articulating the richness and possibility of black communitarian existence as part of God's common purpose for the human race.

Because theology is a human discipline, it must be understood that when black people (or any people) speak of God, it is not God who is speaking, but people attempting to speak of God out of their cultural and

---

[79]Ibid., 85-86.

[80]Statement of the Board of Directors, "The Black Theology Project 1983-1985: Goals, Objectives, Programs, Structures," New York Public Library, Special Collections, Schomburg Center for Research in Black Culture.

social experience.[81] Black liberation theology is an effort to articulate systematic thought of God, Christ, humanity, and community out of black people's struggle for freedom.[82] The presuppositions of black liberation theology explore the conceptual bias that results from socio-economic and political forces that distort the human idea of God and black humanity. Kelly Miller Smith, Sr., remarks,

> Simply put, black theology is the understanding of the experiences of black people in terms of the Christian gospel. It is an elucidation of what we have understood God to be about in our history, and particularly in the history of our struggle against fascist oppression . . . the understanding of God's involvement in the struggle against oppression.[83]

Second, black theology affirms that the "black experience" of survival and liberation are in solidarity with the redemptive and liberating acts of God. The phrase, "black experience," used by black theologians as a source for doing black theology, means the felt, bodily, psycho-social, religious experience and organic action of black human beings in the struggle against oppression. The black experience, in this sense, refers to black people's conscious experience of oppression, how it is internalized in cognitive, intuitive, and religious understanding of the self.

Third, black liberation theology reflects on the black experience in view of God's revelation and disclosure in Jesus Christ. The task of black liberation theology is to interpret how God is a concrete part of the black experience and to articulate the conditions for God's involvement in the particularity of black existence. Jesus Christ is the liberator whose life, death, and resurrection are in solidarity with the black hope for a liberated humanity and future.

Finally, because black liberation theology arises out of the lived experience of black existence, it is accountable to and a servant of the black community. As a servant of the black community, the goal of black liberation theology is to understand the nature and mission of the black

---

[81]Ibid., 2.

[82]James H. Cone, *God of the Oppressed*, 108.

[83]Kelly Miller Smith, Sr., "Religion As A Force In Black America," unpublished paper, Special Collections, Jean and Alexander Heard Library Vanderbilt University, Nashville, TN, 206.

church and to uncover the meaning of Christian symbols that enliven and release the creativity of the church in its praxis and interaction with God. Thus, the task of black liberation theology also is to sensitize the church to the activity of God and to call the church to unite its mission with God's actions and purpose. In a statement of the goals, objectives, and structure of the Black Theology Project, the basic aim of black liberation theology that relates to the black church's social ministry is:

1. To explicate the nature and mission of the black church as understood by its liberationist tradition.

2. To reflect on the contemporary faith and function of the black church and to access its present praxis in view of its nature and mission.

3. To inform the praxis of the black church in view of contemporary sociopolitical issues and the ultimate liberation and justice concerns of faith.

4. To present the black church with a contemporary representation of itself which allow it a means for ongoing self-evaluation and transformation.[84]

Black liberation theology moves between the black church and community; the church proclaims the message, and the message issues into social action reverberating back upon the church's social praxis (action/reflection).[85] Black liberation theology serves as a critical and constructive discipline of reflection on the social praxis of the black church. Social praxis requires a process or method of ministry that engages the black church in continuous theological renewal and authentication of its ministry. Theological reflection on the task of social ministry in the black church is crucial for the renewal and empowerment of black Christians for a liberating ministry.

---

[84]Gayraud S. Wilmore, "Origin and Future of The Black Theology Project: Some Reflections," The Black Theology Project Paper, New York Public Library, Special Collections, Schomburg Center, 13.

[85]Ibid., 12.

In conclusion, without theological renewal of its social ministry, the black church will lose its locus, power, vitality, and vision for social transformation. The praxis of black liberation theology supports the development of a pragmatic spirituality for the black church's social ministry that uses "the gospel and the church to make and to keep life human."[86] The absence of significant theological discourse, its praxis, and political and cultural strategy at the congregational level diminishes the black church's ability to reflect on and develop liberation ministry.[87] A new ministry orientation undergirded by the liberative praxis of black theological thought is a vital need in black churches today.

Contextual Theological Reflection

Another problem that perpetuates the theological crisis of "twoness" in the black church's efforts to do social ministry is the failure to ground theological reflection in contextual thinking. Social oppression manifests itself in poverty, economic depression, poor housing, urban crime, and violence. These contextual factors have an intrinsic bearing on the church's theological perspective and how the church's praxis is shaped.

Theology wears a contextual face and differs from one cultural period to another. As shown in chapter 1, contextual factors in black existence were answered in fundamentally religious ways that undergirded social, political, and economic responses. A decontextualization of theological reflection weakens a serious grappling with the existential particularity of black oppression. In relation to the black church's ministry, decontextualized theological reflection diminishes the ability of the black church to interpret social factors that affect black existence.[88]

As previously argued, all theological thought arises out of contextual experiences in which people struggle to know the meaning of their humanity. Failure to perceive that the black church's theological thought arises out of the contextual experiences of the black community, and not vice versa, results in distortions of church's ecclesial life.[89]

---

[86]Ibid., 156.

[87] Wilmore, "A Revolution Unfulfilled, But Not Invalidated," in James H. Cone, *A Black Theology of Liberation,* 20th anniversary ed., 158.

[88]James H. Cone, *God of the Oppressed,* 108-33.

[89]Peter J. Paris, *Social Teachings of the Black Churches,* 75.

The thesis of this study supports an ecclesial understanding of the black church as an agent for human liberation. Praxis, as understood in the context of the black Christian tradition, suggests that black church ecclesiology be grounded in concepts of the reign of God, that is, relationality and community. This concept challenges black Christians to be agents of social justice and human liberation.

Ecclesial Life in Liberation Praxis

The black church reality participates in the vision of the reign of God. The life of Jesus Christ is the earthly embodiment of that vision. What Jesus did in his life, death, and resurrection was to incarnate the kingdom's vision of creative transformation of the world. In other words, Jesus' ministry was praxis toward the freedom of God's people. Christianity is the cultural expression of this vision filtered through the self-understanding of a particular people's corporate faith and religious experience. Such an understanding of the church's life is what is implied by the term ecclesiology. Thus "black Christianity" is the particular religious and theological appropriation African Americans give to the gospel of Jesus Christ.

In view of its ecclesial history, the black church is seen as an instrument of God's liberation in the world.[90] Wilmore has convincingly argued that the unique challenge of the black church is to use its history, culture, and struggle for freedom to enhance the proclamation of the gospel of Jesus Christ toward total liberation of God's total creation.[91]

Each historical and cultural period requires the church to rethink and reexamine the shape of its life and to adjust its theology and structure to operate more effectively in the social environment in which it finds itself. New complex forms of cultural pluralism and diversity, social stratification, black woman's liberation, and third world poverty are current forces that demand rethinking of the black church's self-understanding.

Avery Dulles contends that, of the five basic ecclesiological models of the church (herald, institution, mystical communion, sacrament, servant), a balanced appropriation of each model should be maintained

---

[90]James H. Cone, *For My People,* 118.
[91]Wilmore, *Black and Presbyterian,* 84.

in the life of the church.[92] Characteristics of all five models can be traced in the black church tradition. Focus here is given to the institutional and servant models of the church. These models, as theoretically interpreted by Dulles, reflect how black churches view themselves and how ecclesial structures in the black churches are designed to accomplish their mission. While the brevity of this discussion will not allow full exploration of these models, this section will say something about the servant and institutional models in relation to liberation praxis in the black church.

The Servant Model

From the perspective of the black church, the servant model of the church emphasizes a liberationist view of praxis. The principle insight of a "praxis in liberation" model of the church is that oppressed humanity and this earth are the objects of God's liberation.[93] William R. Burrows, in *New Ministries: The Global Context*, indicates that ministry performed under the model of Jesus includes both an objective (outer liberation) and subjective (inner liberation) redemptive response to human liberation. Burrows remarks,

> A new mode of being in the world has been made possible by Christ's life, death, and resurrection (objective liberation). A possible mode of being in the world (subjective liberation) becomes actual as believers avail themselves of Christ's transformative power and strive to liberate their brothers and sisters. Thus the church's vocation of social ministry is to extend Christ liberation to whatever oppresses humankind.[94]

Liberation and praxis are inseparably linked in the black church tradition. The black church's involvement in liberation praxis is theologically based upon the conviction that God cares for social victims and

---

[92]Avery Dulles states, "Religious imagery is both functional and cognitive. Cultural changes has produced a crisis of images. Traditional images lose their former hold on people while new images have not yet had time to gain full power." In my opinion the "image of crisis" in the ecclesial life of black churches is perpetuated by the ethical paradox of the black Christian tradition in tension with Euro-Western religious ideology. See Dulles, *Models of the Church* (Garden City, New York: Image Books, 1974) 25.

[93]William R. Burrows, *New Ministries: The Global Context*, 41.

[94]Ibid., 40.

is involved in their struggle for freedom. A liberative praxis focuses on God's love, power, and justice that function among the oppressed for their salvation—salvation from dehumanizing life conditions and salvation to respond fully to God's purposes for humanity.[95]

Kelly Miller Smith, Sr., notes accurately that social realities are profoundly religious matters calling for praxis in liberation. As a black church leader, Smith approached the problem of oppression from within the faith.[96] Smith explains that liberative praxis is "the effort to abolish oppression; this is a work of God and those who do it are truly God's people."[97]

In summary, ecclesiology in the black church is based on: (1) an interpretation of God's purpose for humanity as disclosed in Jesus Christ; (2) an interpretation of God's relationship to social victims and the proclamation of God's activity in their liberation; (3) an interpretation of Jesus Christ, the one in whom God's liberation occurs, as one of the oppressed whose ministry was to the oppressed; (4) correlation of the Christian witness to the struggle and concrete needs of social victims for liberation; and (5) liberation of social victims as a revelation of what God is doing in the world.[98]

Institutional Model

Alongside the black church's liberationist servant image of the church is an institutional model of the church. Dulles states that the church as institution seeks to unite men and women into a well-knit community of conviction, commitment, and hope.[99] The church could not perform its mission without an institutional and structural organization of its internal life.[100] In the black church tradition, the institutional side of the church developed around the charismatic gifts and leadership of the black pastor. In some cases, charismatic black religious leadership effectively organized the internal life of the church in a way that advanced its liberation

---

[95]Luther Smith, *The Mystic as Prophet*, 12.
[96]Kelly Miller Smith, Sr., "Religion as a Force in Black America," 205.
[97]Ibid., 205.
[98]Ibid., 172.
[99]Dulles, *Models of the Church*, 34.
[100]Ibid., 32.

mission and supported institutional integrity. In other cases, institutional integrity deteriorated to institutionalism centered in the power and charismatic gifts of the black pastor.

A leadership posture that supports institutionalism places the black pastor in the position of being a wise manipulator of the church's resources for both the church's institutional survival and the black minister's own survival as leader. Institutionalism in the black church, coupled with the perennial problems of having to face a large community with a myriad of problems and limited resources to solve them, seriously curtails the mobilization and empowerment of black congregations for social ministry.[101]

The black church's institutionalization of the principle of human equality under God has been ambiguously applied in a sectarian, proscriptive doctrinal polity that reduces its members to a condition of passivity, making their membership into a mere appendage of an institutional male-dominated hierarchy. Because of this proscriptive polity in the black church, the integrity of the principle embodied in the black Christian tradition is compromised.

For example, the equality of black women remains an unresolved dilemma in the black church. Black women experience the black church's institutionalism as oppressive and as a contradiction within its liberationist tradition. Institutionalism prevents the black church from transcending the barriers of exclusivism, in terms of black women's equality within the church, and constricts social justice to external forms of equality (equality of rights, social privilege and political power). Yet black Christian tradition promotes "an equality of infinite worth" to be found and achieved through an encounter with God, the source of community.

As previously discussed, in the black church is inseparably linked to a theology of the beloved community or reign of God. As Kelly Miller Smith, Sr., notes: "Protest against injustice is a familiar action of the black community through the church. To separate the political from the spiritual or moral is diametrically opposed to the black church's self-understanding."[102] This fundamental vision of ecclesial life led to the development of four basic models of social ministry in black churches:

---

[101]Floyd Massey and Samuel McKinney, *Administration in the Black Church Perspective* (Valley Forge: Judson Press, 1976) 11.

[102]Kelly Miller Smith, Sr., "Religion as a Force in Black America," 201.

pastoral, prophetic, reformist, and nationalist.[103] Peter Paris maintains that each model demonstrates forms of action and life that were shaped, refined, and preserved by churches.[104] These models will be expanded upon in chapter four. It is important to note how these models shape the black church story and experience in praxis.

In summary, ecclesial praxis in the black church is relational activity (action in reflection) grounded in a liberationist appropriation of the gospel. Correlation of the biblical story, the black Christian tradition and black church experience with the cultural context of black life nurtures an understanding of liberation in praxis toward the end goal of the riegn of God.

---

[103]Peter J. Paris, "The Bible and the Black Churches," 134.
[104]Ibid., 134.

Chapter 3

Method for the Development of Social Ministry in the Black Church

The focus of this chapter is to explore an action-reflection model that awakens the vocation of liberation in the ministry activity of black Christians. The action-reflection model proposed entails a liberation process that involves black Christians in local congregations in "the hermeneutics of the kingdom" by correlation of the black Christian story with the biblical story of liberation. This hermeneutical engagement gives specific attention to the black Christian story of survival and liberation (past and present) as a starting point for dialogue and the raising of questions about the interpretation of biblical texts. The praxis model proposed here is one supported by black liberation theology that seeks to hold together the black Christian story, reflection and action, and inner and outer liberation in the praxis of the black church.

In the black church, praxis emerges out of the communal qualities of the black Christian story and is expressed in various forms of black church worship, music, preaching, song, and testimonies. Liberation praxis must be concerned with the inner and outer dimensions of communal existence, as this represents the core reality of the black Christian story. In other words, it calls for the focus of praxis to be within and without, else, as Gustavo Gutierrez notes, the oppressed "go limping after liberation."

Thomas H. Groome's "shared Christian praxis" model is an appropriate framework for bringing together the black Christian story in dialectical tension with the biblical story of liberation and freedom under God. Groome's shared Christian praxis model of reflection is viewed here from the perspective of the black church's ministry tradition. This praxis model supports the concept of relationality, a concept we believe to be crucial to the praxis of ministry in the black church. In its relational and contextual character, the praxis of ministry demands a commitment to liberation and the building up of persons in community. This commitment to liberation is what we mean by the "praxis of ministry" in the black church.

Praxis of Ministry: Black Church Perspective

Gayraud S. Wilmore's statement mentioned earlier, regarding the task of ministry in the black church, bears repeating because it provides a solid premise for understanding praxis in the black church.

> How can the black churches use the history, culture, and experience of their historic struggle for freedom, to enhance the proclamation of the gospel of Jesus Christ and the manifestation of his power to transform not only Black humanity but the whole human race?[1]

This question calls for what Groome's calls "a praxis way of knowing" that invites critical reflection on the "lived experience" of the black church community.[2] A "praxis way of knowing" refers to the knowledge a church gains through reflection upon its story along with the ministry and the interaction in which it is engaged.[3]

The black church, according to Kelly Miller Smith, Sr., is engaged in the "business of liberation." Its praxis involves the liberation of the oppressed. How has the black church kept liberation as a "praxis way of knowing" alive in its ministry action? Black theologians are returning to the black story of survival and liberation to uncover the power of "praxis in freedom" in the black church tradition. The recovery of the black story in a liberating ministry is crucial for keeping alive "a praxis way of knowing" in the black church. Thomas H. Groome's states that praxis in ministry involves: (1) critical reflection or evaluation on present action,

---

[1]Gayraud S. Wilmore, *Black and Presbyterian: The Heritage and the Hope*, 84.

[2]Thomas H. Groome, *Religious Christian Education: Sharing Our Story and Vision* (San Francisco: Harper & Row, 1980) 185.

[3]James N. Poling and Donald E. Miller, *Foundations for a Practical Theology of Ministry* (Nashville: Abingdon Press, 1985) 65.

(2) critical memory to uncover the past in the present (anamnestic solidarity), and (3) creative imagination to envision the future in the present.[4]

Critical reflection on present ministry action or the lived experience of black Christians will bring to the surface stories of black survival and liberation. These stories, in the words of Prathia Hall-Wynn, teach us "how weakness can survive and overcome oppression. They witness to a freedom faith that starts with black people's understanding of God and how God intends for blacks to be free."[5] In this sense, praxis in liberation is kept alive by the telling of and reflection on the black story. The basic assumptions, beliefs, ideology, and values that shape black people's response to oppression are uncovered in stories. When the hermeneutical meaning and value of the black Christian story is disclosed, persons discover what connects them in liberation ministry. Therefore, in the black church, it is important that stories of oppression be heard; efforts directed toward self-liberation need listening too. Stories of broken dreams due to racial discrimination are important. Black women's experiences of triple oppression (racism, sexism, poverty) need telling. Frustration with powerlessness will surface when these stories are told. Groome convincingly remarks that without the telling of these stories "a praxis way of knowing" does not surface in ministry action, and persons find it difficult to discover what connects them in the praxis of ministry.

Action-Reflection: Praxis in Liberation

What follows is a praxis model that involves recommended steps for group dialogue and action-reflection in developing "a praxis way of knowing" and being among Christians in local black congregations.

---

[4]Thomas H. Groome, *Christian Religious Education*, 185.

[5]This statement was made by Prathia Hall-Wynn during a consultation meeting hosted by the Kelly Miller Smith Institute on African American Church Studies at Vanderbilt Divinity School held in October 1992. This consultation meeting brought together a number of black theologians and church leaders for dialogue regarding a praxis and theological vision for social transformation of the black community.

Step 1. Description of the Church's Present Ministry

The first step involves a description of the present ministry or events in which the group or church is engaged. Present ministry action here means any internal or external ministry activity of the church. This step requires the formation of a group for reflection on the church's present ministry. The goal of this first step is to discover what the present ministry means in the life of individual members. In other words, how does the ministry event support one's basic self-interest, inform faith, values, and religious world view? The goal is to elicit an expression of one's own knowing of that which arises from the person's own lived experience of oppression.[6] The group involved in this reflection seeks to uncover the meaning of the ministry event and its continuing importance for connecting them with each other in liberation.

This step involves "attentiveness to lived experience," or an awareness of stories in context of oppression. In order for people to be connected in ministry, they must become a part of one another's stories and discover the linkage that their story has with other persons involved in the ministry of the church.

The facilitator of this group reflection must be alert to ways to stimulate the storytelling by participants. This reflection may be started by asking such questions as: Why are you involved in this kind of ministry activity? What meaning does this ministry hold for you? How does this ministry serve your self-interest? What can you name in the church that promotes social justice? What is liberating about the current ministry event? These questions or similar ones might open up past stories of oppression that show linkage or indicate why a person may have interest in the present ministry.

Since the publication of James Cone's *God of the Oppressed*, he, as well as other black theologians, has shown greater appreciation for the rich theological content of the black story as expressed in slave narratives, tales, sermons, and songs. As clearly evidenced in Cone's most recent book, *Martin and Malcolm and America: A Dream or A Nightmare*, the personal and corporate biographies of black people are fertile resources for theological reflection on a liberating praxis. In this

---

[6]Thomas Groome, *Christian Religious Education*, 209.

first step of reflection, the group may draw on biographies of liberation that illuminate the meaning of the group's own story.

As Groome warns, the facilitator must guard against projection of abstractions on experiences that are sterile and inaccurate.[7] Stories of lived experiences have multiple meanings that potentially can distort the meaning of the experience itself.[8] The relative character of stories has an ambiguous flux that often confuses the hidden meaning they have for understanding the present. The facilitator must be skillful to alert the group members to the relativity of perspectives, the bias, and self-interest inherent in their stories.[9]

Cone points out that the black story entails two levels of the black experience. First, as Cone notes, there is the story of the people as whole:

> This story goes back to the memories of Africa and the experience of being taken into slavery in North America. It includes the striving of black people to survive the ordeal of servitude and to retain a measure of togetherness. The second level is personal story. Personal story is an account of individual triumphs in struggle.[10]

These stories must be allowed expression in whatever form they appear; and with sensitive prodding and probing, they must proceed to a form of criticism that leads to increased corporate and personal awareness of inner and outer oppression.[11]

This aspect of praxis discloses that which connects people's self-interest and enables the formation of "informed consensus" about the kind of liberation and transformation people seek for their lives.

---

[7]Ibid., 75.
[8]Ibid., 81.
[9]Ibid.
[10]James H. Cone, *God of the Oppressed* (New York: Seabury Books, 1975) 105.
[11]Ibid., 74.

Step 2. Critical Awareness of Participants'
Perspective and Self-Interest

This aspect of shared praxis invites critical reflection on "why the church does what it does, and what are the hopes and the intended consequences of the present ministry action."[12] In the context of this reflection, the word "critical" means the capacity for continuous self-criticism, to become aware of the biases, assumptions, and self-interest that influence one's ministry perspectives and decisions. "Self-criticism includes a method of exploring conceptual bias that results from socio-economic, political, and psychological forces."[13] A principle of self-criticism is needed to guard the group and the church from naive theological assumptions and narrow religious self-serving conclusions regarding the purpose of ministry.

This second step of praxis is aimed at discerning the "liberation going on in the group," attempting to become aware of the reason for its theological and social genesis.[14] The purpose of this reflection is to uncover the self-interest, the faith perspectives, the value in the event itself that led to commitment to the present ministry action. Clarification of self-interest leads to an awareness of people's stories and visions as they are expressed in commitment to the present ministry action.[15] The goal of this praxis response is to discover the norms, social conditioning, and assumptions that are embodied in the present action.[16] This aspect of praxis is both descriptive and normative to discern "what is" (reality) and "what ought to be" (the vision).

Step 3. Correlation of the Biblical Story, the Black
Christian Tradition, and Vision of the Reign of God

The third step of the action-reflection model involves the correlation of the story and vision of the black Christian tradition with the biblical

---

[12]Ibid., 208.
[13]Ibid., 63.
[14]Ibid., 211.
[15]Ibid.
[16]Ibid.

vision of the reign of God. The goal of this reflection is to make clear the group's collective stories and visions (lived ministry experiences) by viewing them in the light of the story and vision of the black Christian tradition. As previously discussed, the black Christian tradition is the particular understanding of the black church regarding our essential humanity under the parenthood and freedom of God.[17] To affirm our essential humanity and that of others in the praxis of ministry, interpreting the black Christian tradition and relating it to the biblical vision of the reign of God are necessary. This step of reflection requires theological analysis to determine how the gospel is commensurate with the realities of black oppression.

Step 4. Dialectic Between the Stories of Participants' Lived Experience and the Biblical Story

The fourth step of reflection involves interpretation of the stories and visions of the group in view of the biblical story and vision.[18] The goal of this reflection is to determine what the black Christian tradition means for the participants' past and present stories (lived experiences). This praxis response involves understanding the dialectical relationship between the inherent value and meaning of the biblical story and vision (as appropriated by the black Christian tradition) and the stories and visions of participants in the church's social ministry. Thomas Groome refers to this process of reflection as "dialectical hermeneutics." Dialectical hermeneutics has three interpretive steps: affirming, refusing, and moving beyond.[19] Groome writes:

> In dialectical hermeneutics of any "text" there is an activity of discerning its truth and what is to be affirmed in it, an activity of discerning the limitations in our understanding of it that are to be refused, and an attempt to move beyond it, carrying forward the truth that was there while adding to it in the new understanding.[20]

---

[17]Peter J. Paris, *Social Teachings of the Black Churches* (Philadelphia: Fortress Press, 1985) 34.

[18]Thomas Groome, *Christian Religious Education*, 217.

[19]Ibid., 196.

[20]Ibid.

The goal of this mode of interpretation is to discover the manner in which God has been present in the lived experiences of the church and the future direction of God's will for the church's liberating ministry.

This process of reflection invites constructive self-criticism and an openness to move beyond limitations in response to God's call to justice. This praxis response is confessional in character and invites reaffirmation of the meaning and value of the biblical story and vision. According to Groome:

> There are times when the Story comes to us as a source of affirmation, encouragement, healing, and hallowing. But knowing that we—in our personal, interpersonal, and social/political lives—are never completely faithful to our faith commitments, there are also times when the Story confronts us, calls us in question, and calls us forward.[21]

The dialectical tension that exists between the participants' stories and the biblical story of liberation brings to consciousness the shortcomings in the church's present praxis and calls its ministry to be more faithful to the tradition.[22]

Step 5. Dialectic Between the Biblical Vision of the Reign of God and the Church's Vision

The fifth step of reflection provides an opportunity for the group and the church to establish perspective for future praxis response in view of past and present ministry action.[23] The goal of this reflection is to uncover the group's self-interest in a critique of stories and visions (lived experiences) inherent in the present vision of ministry. Through this process, the group's social self-interest is uncovered. Correlation of the group's vision with the biblical vision of the reign of God creates a consensus that gives guidance for future ministry decisions. Consensus, in this sense, is "informed consent" grounded theologically and relational in a praxis response for deciding future ministry action. This stage of reflection involves a self-critical principle to enlarge the group's self-interest in

---

[21]Ibid., 217.
[22]Ibid., 220.
[23]Ibid.

view of the ultimate ends of the reign of God. At this stage of the church's reflection, a written vision or mission statement needs to be developed that represents the "informed consent" of the group.

Informed consent in the praxis of liberation is important to the future direction of ministry. It requires the church to interpret and reinterpret its lived experience of oppression in view of the story and vision of the black Christian tradition.[24] This process of interpretation and reinterpretation involves: (1) discernment of God's liberating activity in one's past and present, (2) commitment to God's liberating activity, and (3) development of strategies for cooperating with God's liberating activity.[25] Future ministry decisions should be open to possibilities for social change at various levels of oppression as represented in the lived experience of the group, the larger community, and a global context. The group involved in this reflection should be open to self-criticism and evaluation of its interpretation and social self-interest in view of the church's faith and theological heritage. The goal of this reflection is to determine if the present ministry action and group's self-interest are consistent with God's liberation of persons and communities in the world.[26]

Organization of the church's praxis response around commitment to God's liberating activity in the community and in the world is germane to the action-reflection model proposed here. Commitment to the reign of God requires *metanoia* (change of mind and heart) that invites faithful response to liberation praxis—social justice and love of God by love of neighbor.[27] Only when this commitment is present in the church can leadership be sufficiently organized for performing social ministry.

A social ministry task force or committee—these persons perhaps will be those engaged in the process of shared praxis—should be formed to formulate step-by-step ministry strategies. As the social ministry project is being implemented, the ministry group is in a continuous mode of "action in reflection," to evaluate accomplishments and to determine

---

[24]Edward Wimberly and Anne Streaty Wimberly, *Liberation and Human Wholeness: The Conversion Experiences of Black People in Slavery and Freedom,* (Nashville: Abingdon Press, 1986) 115.

[25]Ibid., 120.

[26]James N. Poling and Donald E. Miller, *Foundation For A Practical Theology of Ministry,* 92.

[27]Ibid., 41.

if the ministry activity supports the liberating value and the anticipated social change.

This process of liberation (reflection/action) requires a socio-cultural and economic analysis of the context in which the ministry event will be performed. A social analysis includes: demographic study of the community; analysis of economic and governmental power base; and analysis of mediating institutions in the community such as churches, colleges, secondary schools, unions, and neighborhood associations. A social analysis is necessary for the development of appropriate strategies for implementing social ministry.

Social Context of Ministry

A church involved in liberative praxis must be cognizant of the social context in which it will carry out social ministry. Because the social context in which most black churches will perform social ministry is within the socio-economic and political environment of the black community, the praxis response will necessarily take on the character of reflection in a context of oppression. An analysis of the church's social context must be done before relevant social ministry can be designed. Social context is inclusive of people's lifestyles and values as well as social structures that restrict and limit human development and freedom. Several social contexts warrant reflection on the development of the black church's social ministry.

1. Context of Culture

The context of culture includes the congregational culture itself as well as the socio-political culture of the community in which it exists. The congregational culture involves the church's developed and distinctive personality that is shaped by its response to a socio-political context. The church's internal culture is "the pattern way of life produced by a people through which its members have guidelines for valuing, believing, and acting."[28] A church must understand and assess its operative culture before deciding about its ministry in the community.

The church's distinctive culture is inclusive of its members' personal histories, that is, their stories, patterns of thinking, feelings, and behaving.[29] The church's socialization and spiritual development patterns represented in a network of group relationships are germane to its culture. These cultural patterns include religious world view, language, family relationships, education, employment, and group affiliation. The cultural pattern and responses within the black church (worship and preaching style, music, ministry actions and decisions) are connected with the social /cultural and political environment of the black community. The socio-cultural context is inextricably interrelated to the church's internal culture and the ministry response the church makes.

2. Analysis of Social Structures

The black church is a mediating institution among its members, the black community, and the social structures that affect black existence. Social structures are representative of public policies, laws, electoral governance, civic ordinances, tax commissions, and school boards in which the benefits of economic and political power are organized and proportioned. Praxis involves reflection on how social structures administer justice in the black community and use power for the benefit of the whole community.

3. Awareness of Various Levels and Forms of Social Oppression

Various forms of oppression manifest themselves when social structures administer injustice. Decades of consistent patterns of social oppression experienced by the African American community have resulted in multiple forms of racial oppression, creating a wide range of social needs. A church must discover the social ministry it is best equipped to provide as a liberating response. The options for appropriate ministry responses

---

[28]Ibid., 110.

[29]James N. Poling and Donald E. Miller, *Foundations for a Practical Theology of Ministry,* 75.

are inexhaustible—housing, education, community development, community organizing, shelter from domestic violence, adoptions, black women's advocacy, single parenting support, prison reform, economic development, and the like.[30] A pressing need that identifies with the self-interest of someone within the church is most often the genesis of a liberating response through social ministry.

Praxis as Service: Black Church Perspective

Social ministry, as defined in this study, is relational, and contextual, and theologically grounded in the biblical vision of the community (reign of God). It is relational because its aim is to build community; it is contextual because it must make relevant contact with the human situation; and it is theological because it seeks unity between Christian social action and God's liberating purposes and activity in the world. These elements in the nature of social ministry can be summarized in the Christological understanding of the word "service."

The conceptual root of ministry is found in the New Testament word *diakonia* (service). Service, in the black church tradition, is not simply social or human services, nor is it limited to worship activities in the sanctuary. Praxis points to service that is liberating, redemptive, and saving as exemplified in activity of Jesus Christ.[31] Kelly Miller Smith, Jr., has asserted that liberative praxis

> is an elucidation of what we have understood God to be about in our history, and particularly in the history of our struggle against fascist oppression . . . the understanding of God's involvement in the struggle against oppression.[32]

While the ministry theme of many churches is to "win souls for Christ," they fail to perceive also that God's salvation is inclusive of

---

[30]See appendix for specific examples.

[31]William R. Burrow, *New Ministries: The Global Context* (New York: Orbis Books, 1981) 55.

[32]Kelly Miller Smith, Sr., "Religion As A Force In Black America," unpublished paper, Special Collections, Jean and Alexander Heard Library Vanderbilt University, Nashville, 206.

justice for social victims. The specific message of the gospel must be made relevant to the social implications of holistic human living, which for the black community includes socio-political realities that, hold life in bondage. Jim Wallis has correctly said that,

> An individualistic understanding of the gospel carries the danger of making salvation into just another commodity that can be consumed for personal fulfillment and self-interest, for a guarantee of happiness, success, moral justification, or whatever else a consumer audience feels it needs. . . . The Christian message is easily co-opted by larger social and political forces that seek to make religion an appendage of the established order.[33]

Socio-political systems tend to oppress life; sin and death most often manifest themselves politically, institutionally, and economically as well as personally.

Prophetic patterns of service take seriously the need to analyze the defects in the social structures that perpetuate dysfunctional lifestyles of individuals.[34] Incorporated into this vision of ministry is the biblical understanding of God's liberating acts of justice. Prophetic ministry tends to be politically engaged and works for systemic social change.

In conclusion, a praxis that is consistent with the ideals of black Christian tradition is needed in local churches to assist person's in their efforts to be faithful to God's justice and in prophetic service to humanity.

---

[33]Jim Wallis, *Agenda for Biblical People* (New York: Harper & Row, 1976) 31.
[34]Ibid., 42.

Chapter 4

Black Religious Leadership and Social Ministry

Black religious leadership is a unique phenomenon in the history of the black church. Its importance to black people's quest for social power and liberation has not been fully documented and accounted for.[1] The Lincoln and Mamiya study suggests the need for a realistic reassessment of the black religious situation that takes into account what black church leaders have been doing and are doing to achieve liberation in the black community.[2] The black pastor, as religious and civic leader, is the most visible and active agent in the social ministry of black churches. How black churches have developed and performed social ministry cannot be understood without an assessment of the relationship between the black pastor and the black church.

Ministry committed to human liberation and the *telos* of community, as previously argued in this study, is a mutual process.[3] Leadership is an essential component of this mutual process of praxis in the black church. Its principle task is to nurture an alternative consciousness from the dominant culture and to evoke participation in God's liberating activity.[4] Social ministry requires leadership that is called and trained to serve the church in its liberating activities, in its social and ecumenical relationships, and in its social praxis and mission in the world. What can black pastors do to cultivate the praxis of liberation in the black church's

---

[1]Lincoln and Mamiya, *The Black Church in the African American Experience* (Durham: Duke University Press, 1991) 161.

[2]Ibid., 161.

[3]Paulo Freire, *Pedagogy of the Oppressed,* (New York: Continuum Publishing Company, 1990) 5.

[4]Walter Brueggemann, *Prophetic Imagination* (Philadelphia: Fortress Press, 1978) 13.

ministry efforts? In fulfilling the function of liberation praxis, what is the black pastor's central role?

The principle focus of this discussion is an exploration of how leadership styles of black pastors empower or delimit local congregation liberation praxis and social ministry. Several leadership issues and problems are discussed regarding black pastors as leaders of black churches' liberating ministry. This chapter analyzes several leadership styles that characterize black religious leaders in their efforts to lead the black churches as change agents for the achievement of social justice. The topics discussed are: (1) black religious leadership and the response to oppression, (2) traits of black religious leadership, (3) problems and issues of black religious leadership, (4) black religious leadership and communal power, and (5) black religious leadership and liberation praxis.

Black Religious Leadership and the Response to Oppression

Historically, the black community's most effective leaders have been nurtured in the "cultural womb" of the black church.[5] What can be said about the black church can also be said of its leadership. In response to racial oppression, protest and passivity, radicalism and moderation, activism and resignation have characterized both the black churches and their pastors.[6] Black religious leadership is inextricably bound up with the social phenomenon of racism and all its social manifestations of oppression. Peter J. Paris has argued:

> There can be no adequate inquiry into the nature of the [black religious leaders] apart from an understanding of the racist character of the social order that has constituted the fundamental conditions for their emergence and dominant reason for their endurance.[7]

---

[5]Lincoln and Mamiya, *The Black Church in the African American Experience*, 8.

[6]Archie Smith, Jr., "The Relational Self in the Black Church: From Bondage to Challenge" in *Changing Views of the Human Condition*, ed. Paul W. Pruyser (Macon, GA: Mercer Press, 1987) 138.

[7]Peter J. Paris, "The Social Teachings of the Black Churches: A Prolegomenon,"

Thus, the basic challenge of black pastors has been the engagement of black people in the struggle against social oppression created by the practice of racism, and the mobilization of the congregation's resources in the common purpose of liberation.[8] Black pastors have met this challenge by functioning as charismatic leaders within the indigenous culture of the black church.

Black religious leadership has played a vital role in black people's survival of slavery, race powerlessness during Reconstruction-era politics, segregation and employment discrimination during the Civil Rights movement, and institutional racism in the post-Martin Luther King, Jr., era.[9] Acccording to Kelly Miller Smith, Jr., during these periods of social crisis black religious leaders developed indigenous ministry responses in the following ways:

(1) Development of distinctive worship, preaching, and leadership styles that foster communal and group identity.

(2) Formation of action groups, committees or ministries within the organizational structure of the church.

(3) Less structured, impromptu responses to social crises such as boycotts, petitions, marches or other forms of direct action, mass meeting, etc.

---

paper presented to the Society of Christian Ethics, 1980.

[8]The "authentic needs" of black people have always been inextricably associated with the quest for liberation. Black religious leadership as expressed in and through the black church, without the necessary perspective and focus of liberation, is ephemeral in its relevance to the black community. In fact, Calvin Marshall states, "No institution [or expression of leadership] needs to exist in the midst of black people unless it is inextricably bound to the liberation struggle of our people." See Calvin B. Marshall, "The Black Church—Its Mission Is Liberation," *The Black Scholar* 2 (December 1970): 13-19.

[9]There is little or no disagreement among scholars of the black religious experience that the black church has been the source and center for the development of the black community's most effective and gifted leaders. Gayraud S. Wilmore states that "born in protest, tested in adversity, led by eloquent and courageous preachers, the black church was the cutting edge of the freedom movement during most of the nineteenth century." See Gayraud S. Wilmore, *Black Religion and Black Radicalism,* 2d ed (New York: Orbis Books, 1983) 95.

(4) Active support of and involvement in collective action on the part of the churches and/or other black community agencies and efforts.[10]

These leaders' initiatives propelled the black community into social action that enabled it "to live in a culture of oppression without being crushed by it."[11] Through the agency of the black church, black religious leaders have maintained the nexus between the black religious experience, prophetic response, and social transformation.[12] Black people have not hesitated to follow persuasive leadership (good or bad) that fulfilled their psychological hungers for freedom and articulated an alternative vision for their liberation. The quest for liberation goes to the deepest roots of the tradition of black religious leadership and the people they seek to lead. Black people have made black religious leaders the trustees of their hopes and aspirations for a liberated future. Many black pastors have met this leadership challenge with courage and imagination, helping social victims deal with a "painful present" (the world as it is), and fostering in them hope for a "radiant future" for a non-oppressed world (the world as it should be).

The quality of leadership the black church successfully developed in its past is now needed to respond to current social crisis in the black community. In view of what Lerone Bennett described in *The Crisis Magazine* as "the crisis of the black spirit," and what Archie Smith, Jr., describes as the "crisis of modernity," a reassessment of traditional leadership models in the black church is needed. As early as 1977, Bennett saw the crisis of the black spirit developing.

We have come to a great fork in the road of black destiny. The signs of crisis are everywhere. The homicide rate in the black community has reached such an astronomical rate that young black males are rapidly becoming an endangered species. And this alarming development is only an extreme manifestation of the anger and frustration of hundreds of thousands of black youth who have given up hope and see no reason

---

[10]Kelly Miller Smith, Sr., "Religion As a Force In Black America," in *The State of Black America, 1982,* ed. James D. Williams (New York: The National Urban League, 1982) 203.

[11]Ibid., 204.

[12]Luther Smith, *Howard Thurman: The Mystic as Prophet* (New York: University Press of America, 1981) 166.

for accepting the discipline required for achievement and excellence. We are losing a whole generation of people. And this fact, which is cultural, political and economic at the same time, constitutes the gravest challenge [the black church] has faced in this country since the end of slavery.[13]

In analyzing the "crisis of modernity," Archie Smith, Jr., comments:

Modern culture, rather than liberating people for self-determination and responsible communal existence, has increased a sense of moral malaise, alienation, and despair. It has diminished the chief human capacities (namely, freedom, reason, and love) for critically reflecting upon [the black] situation and transforming a repressive social order.[14]

The question facing the leadership of the contemporary black church is whether its resources and tradition can adequately organize the liberation activity of the black community and minister to oppressed people in a secular, highly differentiated, pluralistic, and technological society.[15] To respond to the social crisis described by Lerone Bennett and Archie Smith, Jr., black church leaders must do serious strategic and tactical reflection on models of effective leadership which can empower black churches for liberation praxis leading to social transformation.[16]

In his assessment of "The Crisis of Black Leadership," Cornel West indicates that the social crisis of the black community calls for a reassessment of black religious leadership. West explains:

The social crises of the black community calls for a reassessment of religious leadership that has disfigured, deformed, and devastated African Americans such that the resources for collective and critical

---

[13]Lerone Bennett, "The Crisis of the Black Spirit," *Ebony Magazine.* (October 1977): 142.

[14]Archie Smith, Jr., "The Relational Self in the Black Church: From Bondage to Challenge" in *Changing Views of the Human Condition,* ed. Paul W. Pruyser (Macon, GA: Mercer University Press, 1987) 136-53.

[15]Ibid., 28.

[16]Cornel West, "The Crisis of Black Leadership," *Black America Magazine* (April 1989): 25.

consciousness, moral commitment, and courageous engagement are vastly underdeveloped.[17]

I concur with this assessment, and I further contend that collective and critical consciousness, moral commitment, and courageous engagement are indispensable leadership characteristics needed for effective leaders in the liberation ministry of the contemporary black church. West further observes: "Quality leadership is not created in a vacuum but comes from deeply-bred traditions that shape and mold talented and gifted persons."[18] As an interpreter of the black Christian tradition and as visionary of the churches ministry in the world, the black pastor must cultivate a collective liberating consciousness and develop skills for organizing the church's shared praxis ministry.

Traits of Black Religious Leadership

Most literature written about black religious leaders either is historical in nature or deals with the singular facet of the black preaching tradition. Scant attention, however, is given to black religious leaders as a source of empowerment for the churches' social ministry. This is particularly true regarding the leadership of the black pastor as an organizer of a church's ministry, and as community activist and leader. Charles S. Rooks has noted in his article, "Toward The Promised Land," that preaching is the chief characteristic of the black pastor's leadership skills and role as builder of community.[19] Because of this phenomenon in black churches, black pastors are sought more for their preaching ability than for their ability to organize the church's social ministry. This lack of emphasis has produced a poverty in knowledge regarding leadership strategies employed by black pastors for designing and structuring social

---

[17]I concur with Cornel West that the leadership crisis in the black community is political, intellectual, as well as religious. West states, "There has not been a time in the history of black people in this country when the quantity of politicians and intellectuals was so great, yet the quality of both groups has been so low." See "The Crisis of Black Leadership," 22-25.

[18]Ibid., 25.

[19]Charles Rooks, "Toward The Promised Land: An Analysis of The Religious Experience of Black Americans," *The Black Church* 2 (January 1972): 16.

ministry. Thus, we know more about the black prophetic preaching tradition than we do about leadership strategies use to organized ministry in response to social problems.

To facilitate our effort to identify the particular traits of black religious leadership necessary to fulfill the black pastor's role as organizer of the church's social ministry, the ministry career of Kelly Miller Smith, Sr., is lifted up as a model for reflection.[20]

Smith organized the Nashville black churches for public policy change during the student sit-in movement in the 1960s. The role he played as president of the National Council of Black Churchmen in negotiating social justice remediation for victims of oppression attest to his skills as a manager of the church's social ministry, community organizer and activist.

A study of the Nashville student movement indicates that during the 1960s Smith was probably considered the most influential of the city's black leaders.[21] John Lewis, a student at the American Baptist Theological Seminary during the period of the student sit-in movement, now a member of the United States Congress, speaks of Smith's influence as critical to the success of the movement:

> First Baptist Church . . . became a rallying point, it became the meeting place where students, young people, community leaders, could meet and discuss, debate and argue what the city should become. Kelly's ministry at the church and his leadership in the community went hand in hand. He had a tremendous influence over almost everything that was taking place in the city of Nashville, in the black community.[22]

---

[20]This study has referred frequently to Smith's concept of liberation praxis in the black church. In these additional comments, Smith's approach to social ministry is described in terms of his praxis skills—civic and religious leadership qualities for which he was admired. The career of Kelly Miller Smith, Sr., who pastored the historic First Baptist Church Capitol, Nashville, Tennessee for thirty-three years, is remembered for his leadership skills in organizing liberation ministry in the black community of Nashville, Tennessee. He was a profound, prophetic, gifted charismatic "social crisis preacher" who also was a skillful community organizer and liberation strategist.

[21]David E. Sumner, "The Local Press and The Nashville Student Movement, 1960," (Ph.D. diss., University of Tennessee, 1989) 21.

[22]Aldon Morris, *The Origin of the Civil Rights Movement* (New York: Free Press, Collier Macmillian, 1984) 175.

As president and founder of the Nashville Christian Leadership Conference, an affiliate of the Southern Christian Leadership Conference, Smith strategically organized the Nashville black community for direct non-violent action. David E. Sumner notes:

> When Martin Luther King, Jr., spoke in Nashville on April 20, 1960, the civil rights leader praised the Nashville initiative as "the best organized and the most disciplined in the Southland" and said the Nashville students had a "better understanding of the philosophy of the nonviolence movement than any other group."[23]

As a religious leader, Smith was civically and politically alert to the resources in the community and developed strong ecumenical and institutional ties he called for during the Nashville sit-in movement. During this period, Smith adopted the nonviolent praxis of Martin Luther King's movement and pull together a network of people for its successful implementation in the city of Nashville. Smith appointed James Lawson, who was a field secretary for the Fellowship of Reconciliation and a student at Vanderbilt Divinity School, to chair the Nashville Christian Leadership Committee's "Project Committee" which was organized to train students in nonviolent principles.[24] Smith's church served as the meeting place for action in reflection on the activities of the student sit-ins. Many who had contact with the ministry of Smith viewed him as a religious leader who possessed the leadership qualities described by Cornel West—"critical and collective consciousness, moral commitment and courageous engagement." Smith did not embody these qualities in any perfect way, but he used his charismatic gifts in a prophetic and pastoral manner, luring his church and the community to embrace the Christian activism and social ministry he effectively practiced.

A chief weakness of charismatic leaders is that they create a dependency in the community upon them. When they are no longer able to provide primary leadership, the community finds it difficult to decide its future. Because black charismatic leaders, like Smith, become passionately involved in fighting the social evils of racism and absorbed

---

[23]Ibid., 20.
[24]Ibid., 22.

with developing a following for social action, creating a great dependency upon their leadership is difficult to avoid.

To the disadvantage of sustained liberation activity in the black community, action in reflection has not been firmly planted in the black churches under charismatic leaders. As James Cone explains, charismatic leaders cannot liberate black people from social misery. Social victims must be empowered to liberate themselves through sincere commitment to the cause of justice and freedom.[25] Smith showed sensitivity to this problem by appointing a social action committee for the purpose of reflecting on the social ministry of First Baptist Church Capitol Hill. This social action committee was responsible for planning and implementing strategies for the First Baptist ministry action.[26]

Smith's leadership was informed by a keen theological mind that understood the relationship between religious experience and political awareness. Smith was a liberationist/preacher/scholar. The theological and practical wisdom that shaped Smith's ecclesiology and guided his liberation praxis contributed to the development of collective and critical consciousness at a crucial period in the city of Nashville. Charismatic and pastoral qualities were admired traits in Smith's leadership style that people trusted and followed. In his essay "The Portrait of a Prophet," Peter J. Paris observes:

> Like all black religious leaders, Kelly Miller Smith's ministry was characterized by many diverse functions, offices and associations. But, unlike many, Smith's leadership, more often than not, produced results. He was able to mobilize people around issues and inspire them to become actively involved.[27]

Paris further states:

---

[25]James Cone, *Martin and Malcolm and American: A Dream or a Nightmare* (New York: Orbis Books, 1991) 315.

[26]"The Kelly Miller Smith, Sr., Papers," Box 50, file 16-17 Special Collections, Jean and Alexander Heard Library, Vanderbilt University, 1989.

[27]Peter J. Paris, "Introduction to the Kelly Miller Smith Papers," arranged and described by Marcia Riggs, Special Collections Jean and Alexander Heard Library, Vanderbilt University, Nashville, 1989, 9.

He seemed always to be calling meetings of one kind or another for purposes of institutional nurture and evaluation, often to start new organizations as a response to some pressing need. Kelly Miller Smith's ministry clearly demonstrates the integral relation between the church and community at large. His ministry integrated prophetic criticism and pastoral care in all his activities, thus reflecting authentic ministry in the black Christian tradition.[28]

Pastoral care, for Smith, was approached within social structures. Likewise the black minister, as pastor and counselor, has access to the inner lives of people and can, therefore, be especially effective in confronting difficult issues and suggesting directions when necessary to effect solution to some social problems. In the Kelly Miller Smith Research Collection, many sermons exhibit balanced treatment of the inner and outer dimensions of liberation, that is, prophetic and pastoral responses to social problems. Smith's sermons discussed severe social crisis with prophetic precision and provided hope for overcoming the crisis, externally and internally. In the sermons "The Creative Crisis," "Something Within," "The Quest for Inner Unity," and "Cry from the Streets," Smith is sensitive to what Howard Thurman called "the journey inward and outward." These sermons gave listeners a clue to the "grain in the pattern of their wood," and told them how to deal inwardly and outwardly with the contradictions of the black existence. Leadership traits characteristic of Smith are evident in the styles of black religious leaders at various levels of Christian social activism throughout the black community. The traits of moral courage, social consciousness and commitment, and the ability to reflect theologically upon social crisis are indispensable for the praxis of ministry. The black pastor has almost limitless opportunities to cause critically needed social change.

---

[28]Ibid., 9.

Kelly Miller Smith, Sr.'s View of Religious Leadership

Kelly Miller Smith, Sr.'s view of the importance of black religious leadership is stated in an unpublished article entitled "Religion As a Force In Black America." In that article Smith noted:

> The extent to which a given black church fulfills its responsibility as the primary agency of the black community is dependent, in large measure, on the vision and leadership qualities of the pastor. The potential of black religious leadership is overwhelming in terms of the current needs of the black community. Perhaps more than anyone else in American society, the black pastor can help black people to survive economically, psychologically and spiritually through the current devastating crises.[29]

Black religious leaders must serve as a conduit for fulfilling the black church's social responsibility to social victims, according to Smith. The pursuit of social remediation is the proper business of the black church's leadership.[30]

Smith deemed it crucial for black churches to raise the question: "Is the minister always a leader?" Smith states that this question can be answered affirmatively if a leader is simply one who has followers.[31] In response to this question, Smith makes a sharp distinction between "black leaders" and "leading blacks." Smith makes this distinction based on Charles Hamilton's analysis of black leadership:

> When one uses the term "black leader," the reference is to two things. "Black" refers to racial identity; "leader" refers to a role. When used together, the words take on an additional meaning: one who is racially black in a leadership role and who speaks and acts on matters of specific concern to black people as a direct purpose of occupying that

---

[29]Kelly Miller Smith, Sr., "Religion as a Force In Black America," in *The State of Black America, 1982,* ed. James D. Williams (New York: The National Urban League, 1982) 24.

[30]Ibid., 205.

[31]Ibid., 222.

role. Thus, "black leaders" refers to racial and role characteristics, but also to issue orientation.[32]

Smith notes that black ministers who are religious leaders, but who do not act politically or civically for the liberation of the black community, are blacks in leadership roles, but they are not black leaders. Black ministers, says Smith,

> should be "internal/external" leaders who understand and perform their functions as pastor of a congregation as well as accept and carry forward leadership responsibilities in the community on behalf of fellow blacks. In short, the need is for an increase in the number of "black religious leaders."[33]

In Smith's view, black religious leadership is a powerful resource for organizing social ministry in the black church.

I define black religious leadership as (1) the effective exercise of one's ability to communicate the values of the black Christian tradition and (2) one's ability to act to mobilize people and resources toward the accomplishment of specific social ministry and liberation goals. The task of black religious leadership is to organize the power and resources of the church around the vision of a transformed humanity and earth (the reign of God or beloved community). To fulfill the task of leadership for the church's social ministry, the black pastor must have: (1) moral commitment, (2) community vision, (3) social consciousness, and (4) theological understanding of the black Christian tradition. What follows is the application of this understanding of black religious leadership to the concept of ministry as shared praxis. First, it is important to note problems inherent in traditional black religious leadership models that prevent the development of a ministry process of shared praxis.

---

[32]Ibid., 222.
[33]Ibid., 223.

Black Religious Leadership: Problems and Issues

The Lincoln and Mamiya study indicates that there is not a consensus among clergy regarding the major problem confronting the leadership of the black church. Of the 1,218 clergy persons who responded to the survey, "Clergy Views of the Church's Major Problem," 103 (4.8 percent) felt that leadership was the major problem and 62 (2.9 percent) felt that uneducated or non-trained clergy was the major problem.

An African Methodist Episcopal pastor responded to the Lincoln and Mamiya survey by saying, "I believe the primary problem facing the church today is the struggle to hammer out a course of action. A theological and philosophical outlook that will reflect a guidance toward the future liberation it projects."[34] I concur with this perspective and see the struggle for a course of action as a leadership issue that challenges the black church to turn to collective and inclusive models of leadership demanded by the current social crisis, multiple self-interests, and diversity present in the black community.

The problems and issues associated with black religious leadership manifest themselves in the leadership styles of contemporary black pastors. In one sense, black religious leadership has been and is a "splendored and splintered thing."[35] In its splendor, black religious leadership is characterized by what C. Eric Lincoln calls the "peculiar genius of the black preacher."

Perhaps the peculiar genius of the black preacher derives from the fact that he has never been far from the people. He rose from among them.

---

[34]Lincoln and Mamiya, *The Black Church in the African American Experience*, 396.

[35]Walter E. Fluker used this phrase to depict the complex nature of the moral and ethical dimensions of the black community as being a "many splendored and splintered thing." This perspective is no less true of black religious leadership and its various responses to the social challenges of racism. See Walter Fluker, *They Look for A City: A Comparative Study of the Ideal of Community in the Thought of Howard Thurman and Martin Luther King, Jr.*, (New York: University Press of American, 1989) 11; and Peter J. Paris, *Black Leaders In Conflict:Joseph H. Jackson, Martin Luther King, Jr., Malcolm X, Adam Clayton Powell, Jr.*, (New York: The Pilgrim Press, 1978) 13.

... When he made good as a preacher, the community shared in his accomplishments, and when they rewarded him for his faithfulness, it was a vicarious expression of the satisfaction the people felt with their own attainments. He was more than a leader and pastor, he was the projection of the people themselves, coping with adversity, symbolizing their success, denouncing their oppressors in clever metaphor and scriptural selection, and moving them on toward that day of Jubilee that would be their liberation.[36]

The creative expression of this "peculiar genius" both within and beyond the black church has produced "world class" intellectual, political and religious leadership. The careers of Nat Turner; Sojourner Truth; Fanny Lou Hammer; Daniel Payne; Richard Allen; Henry McNeal Turner; Mary Church Terrell; J. Alfred Smith, Sr.; Nannie Helen Buroughs; Jarena Lee; Amanda Berry Smith; Anna Julia Cooper; Mary McCloud Bethune; Marcus Garvey; W. E. B. DuBois; Booker T. Washington; Ida B. Wells; Adam Clayton Powell, Sr., and Jr.; Martin Luther King, Sr., and Jr.; Malcolm X; Joseph H. Jackson; Sandy F. Ray; William Holmes Borders; Kelly Smith, Sr.; Fred Lofton; Charles Adams; T. J. Jemison; Leon Sullivan; Samuel DeWitt Proctor; Prathia Hall Wynn; and Kelly Miller Smith, Sr., are examples par excellence of this tradition, to name only a few. Unheralded black prophetic preachers like the late Brady Johnson, who was pastor of the Spring Hill Baptist Church for forty years, could be added to this list.

Scholars of the black church tradition generally agree that the church could not have captured the central place in the black community without the intelligent and creative leadership of the black preacher.[37] As noted by Lincoln and Mamiya, "The black church [and its leadership] is no more and no less than the black people who comprise it, and mirrors the imagination, the interest, and the sense of urgency of the black community it serves and symbolizes."[38]

Alongside of its splendor, however, exists a splintered condition in the black religious leadership tradition. Peter J. Paris has shown that

---

[36]C. Eric Lincoln, ed., *The Black Experience in Religion: A Book of Readings* (New York: Anchor Books, 1974) 85.

[37]Charles Shellby Rooks, "Toward The Promised Land: An Analysis of the Religious Experience of Black Americans," *The Black Church* 2 (1972): 10.

[38]Lincoln and Mamiya, *The Black Church in the African American Experience,* 60.

black religious leaders have a history of conflict, not only with those who promote racism, but with themselves as well. Paris explains, "They have agreed that racism should be opposed but they have vigorously disagreed on the form the opposition should take."[39]

The persistence of conflict among black religious leaders created what James Melvin Washington calls a "frustrated fellowship" in the life of the black church. The frustrated fellowship to which Washington refers involves a three-fold problem: (1) conflicting styles, (2) uncritical embrace of white religious ideology, and (3) the charismatic polity and one-man rule authority of black church religious leaders. In his analysis of black national Baptist leadership, Washington states:

> Black Baptist uncritically embraced Americanist ideology of works of righteousness. Although this yearning for self-determination is evident throughout black Baptist history, it achieved a consummate expression during Joseph Harrison Jackson's administration of the National Baptist Convention. The price black Baptist paid, however, was to be remembered as a reactionary institution that refused to take a prophetic stance in support of Martin Luther King's historic Civil Rights movement. They could produce prophets (King was a member of the National Baptist Convention but later split from it to form the Progressive National Convention) but they were still in bondage to a charismatic polity that depended on what Edward L. Wheeler correctly calls "one-man rule." [40]

I support Washington's analysis and contend that the "one-man rule" and "charismatic polity" in the leadership tradition of the black church resulted in not only a "frustrated fellowship" but a leadership crisis that hindered the empowerment of the black church for liberation ministry.

---

[39]Peter J. Paris, *Black Leaders in Conflict: Joseph H. Jackson, Martin Luther King Jr., Malcolm X, Adam Clayton Powell, Jr.,* 12.

[40]James Melvin Washington, *Frustrated Fellowship: The Baptist Quest for Social Power* (Macon, GA: Mercer Press, 1986) xvii. The title of Washington's book was borrowed from a statement made by Dr. Sandy F. Ray who in a lecture at Yale Divinity School referred to "the national life of black Baptist as a 'frustrated fellowship' whose unfocused collective power is one of the greatest tragedies of African American religious history."

While black pastors have served as the vanguard of black people's quest for freedom, their role as organizers of the church's liberation ministry has suffered much ambiguity and abstruseness, causing the development of reactionary leadership patterns that placed many ministry initiatives at variance with the end-goal and vision of the black Christian tradition. One of the continuing paradoxes of black religious leaders, as the trustees of the religious aspirations of black people, is that they, in Gayraud Wilmore's words,

> are at once the most reactionary and the most radical leaders, the most imbued with the essence of black religion and the values of white religion and yet the most proud, the most independent persons in the black community.[41]

This ambiguous character of black religious leadership has developed an internal culture in the black churches that sanctions ineffective leadership styles and approaches to social ministry. James Cone appropriately contends:

> The black church has been radical, serving as the most important instrument of black liberation, but it has also been one of the most conservative institutions in the black community.[42]

Cone continues:

> The black church produced Martin Luther King, who creatively joined black religion with the struggle for justice; but it has also produced many Joseph H. Jacksons whose views on Christianity and politics were as conservative as King's were radical.[43]

This problem in black religious leadership served as the basis for the development of diverse leadership styles that perpetuated the pattern of "charismatic polity" and "one-man rule" in decision-making regarding

---

[41]Gayraud S. Wilmore, *Black Religion and Black Radicalism,* 2d ed. (New York: Orbis Books, 1984) x.

[42]James H. Cone, *For My People: Black Theology and the Black Church* (Maryknoll, New York: Orbis Books, 1984) 100.

[43]Ibid., 100.

governance and ministry formation in the black church. When the church's ministry is under the influence of a "charismatic polity"—"one-man rule" leadership style—dominance, bureaucratic control, top-down administrative decision-making characterizes the church's ministry process. Contemporary black churches must assess patterns of leadership that affect the way in which ministry decisions are made and implemented. This assessment should include but not be limited to: (1) an assessment of traditional black religious leadership styles, (2) an assessment of communal power, and (3) theological reorientation based on communal values and faith perspectives inherent in the black Christian tradition.

Styles of Black Religious Leadership

For the purpose of this discussion, four models of leadership are discussed as they relate to the liberation praxis in the black church: pastoral, prophetic, reformist, and nationalistic. Characteristics of each of these leadership models appear in the liberation perspectives of black pastors and shape their approach to social ministry. Black religious leaders have combined various aspects of each leadership model in the quest for social power and social justice. Elements of prophetic radicalism are sometimes combined with the pastoral model, nationalistic strategies overlap with reformist interest, and reformists share some of the views of prophetic radicalism. Extended research needs to be done to determine what forms of pastoral, prophetic, reformist, and nationalist leadership have been effective in organizing the black church and community for moral and social change.

The argument here is that the effectiveness of various models of black religious leadership is based on moral accountability to the black community. Moral accountability is inseparably linked to the ethics and values inherent in the aspirations and hopes of the black church and community. Moral leadership in the black church reflects effective response to black suffering and human need in a way that maintains a common set of values, moral ideals, and beliefs that mobilize people for shared participation in responsible praxis.

Pastoral Model

What type of pastoral support is needed to assist the development of liberation praxis in the black church? Pastoral assistance toward the survival and liberation of oppressed social victims is an undertaking of enormous responsibility. Black pastors have fulfilled this responsibility using a variety of approaches. In most cases, black clergy view the pastoral function in light of the social demands of ministry in the black community. Others carry out pastoral activity from an otherworldly religious orientation. The primary objective of pastoral activity in the black church—to comfort and to console those battered by life's adverse circumstances—must be done with a view toward holistic transformation of black life.

Pastors whose vision of ministry is nurtured exclusively in an otherworldly piety often find prophetic activism in conflict with an emphasis on personal salvation. When confronting the critical social and spiritual needs of persons who have been abused by oppressive power structures, pastors soon discover that the negative and legalistic notion of a hell or heaven option for salvation is religious nonsense. As J. DeOtis Roberts notes,

> In crisis situations many [pastors] are concerned with the inerrancy of Scripture and the future rapture. Those who do get involved from the fundamentalist side sanctify the political status quo.[44]

The political status quo for the black community means no change in the collective social evil and group suffering of oppressed persons.

Liberating praxis demands that black pastors care for oppressed persons within social structures that negatively affect the development of people's lives. Pastoral ministry viewed mainly in terms of private spirituality internalizes liberation for social change to the extent that pastoral action does not seriously challenge the external structures of social oppression. This pastoral style is basically "transactional"

---

[44]J. DeOtis Roberts, *Black Theology in Dialogue* (Philadelphia: The Westminster Press, 1991) 14.

(exchange of promises for loyalty), which encourages gradualism, endurance, and patience during conflict and adversity. It locks a local church into an unconscious maintenance of the status quo. Black pastors who identified with the extremes of this pastoral style mainly focus upon institutional maintenance, constructing buildings, and raising budgets. In other words, the pastoral energies of these ministers are expended more in managing institutional and organizational concerns than in managing the church's liberating ministry.

A responsible pastoral approach to the social problems of oppressed persons is to enlist justice for the oppressed in the service of love. A litany of social woes, families bereft by domestic violence, and economic crises require black pastors to find a method to provide sustained pastoral care for meeting inner and outer liberation needs. In the care of social victims, attention must be given to how collective evils increase the personal suffering of oppressed persons and to how faith in God enables these people to find psychological and spiritual health that helps them deal with social problems. Social problems manifest themselves in the personal struggles of the black family. Private troubles of oppressed persons are intertwined with social structures that deny justice and freedom.

In the praxis of liberation, pastoral ministry must be holistic in helping and leading oppressed persons to affirm inward acts of liberation as well as alternatives to social justice. In this sense, pastoral ministry is prophetic commitment and service. Pastoral ministry must deal with the reality of oppression in a way that makes life more human for persons who look to their minister for care. Black pastors have discovered that the help social victims need goes beyond support in various forms of social services and human aid. Human goodwill expressed toward social victims is not sufficient to develop the consciousness necessary for continuous acts of inward and outward liberation.[45] To encourage self-help, self-improvement, and private spirituality at the expense of not dealing with structural evils falls short of the responsible praxis called for in oppressed communities. As one who stands in and for social victims, the black pastor's task is to hold before the church and community the praxis vision of love in the service of justice and freedom.

---

[45]Peter J. Paris, "The Black Churches and the Bible," 135.

With the pastoral emphasis on the liberating praxis, black pastors are in solidarity with social victims, keeping hopes for the inner and outer liberation in perspective. Black pastors often are the first persons to hear stories that deal with inner and outer realities of oppression. These stories represent an opportunity for dialogue (action in reflection) that involves both the pastor and oppressed persons in liberating praxis. Pastoral response to the social and spiritual pain of social victims would be greatly enhanced by such dialogue.

Love is an essential element in any effective form of action in reflection (dialogue) in pastoral ministry. Love, as defined by the demands of justice, holds action and reflection together in pastoral responses to oppression. When action is separated from reflection or when reflection is unrelated to action, a critical understanding cannot be gained on the context of oppression in which a pastoral response is demanded.[46]

In conclusion, the pastoral function must be grounded in a praxis inferred by love and justice, which is the moral content of pastoral activity. As Paulo Freire notes, "No matter where the oppressed are found, the act of love is commitment to their [quest for justice]—the cause of liberation."[47] Pastoral action in liberating praxis requires ongoing reflection on inner and outer dimensions of love and justice as they relate to the care of oppressed persons. In other words, pastoral ministry in the black church tradition must be done in the service of love and justice.

Prophetic Model

The prophetic model of leadership seeks to reveal the contradictions inherent in the life of the community and dominant culture and to clarify the ethical vision of justice in situations of human oppression.[48] The prophetic dimension of liberation ministry seeks to integrate the demands of love, power, and justice into the life of the community itself and upon

---

[46]Archie Smith, Jr., *The Relational Self: Ethics and Therapy from a Black Church Perspective*, 127.

[47]Paulo Freire, *Pedagogy of the Oppressed*, 77-78.

[48] Peter J. Paris, "The Bible and The Black Churches," 137.

the dominant culture.[49] With the emphasis on praxis in liberation, prophetic leadership assists people in identifying and opposing social evil that afflicts them.

In his analysis of prophetic ministry, Walter Brueggemann articulates the basic perspective that this writer believes to be the prophetic dimension of a shared praxis vision of ministry. Brueggemann's thesis declares: "The prophetic task of ministry is to nurture, nourish, and evoke a consciousness in perception alternative to the consciousness and perception of the dominant culture around us."[50] This prophetic task involves passionate advocacy of God's justice through the agency of love. This prophetic stance cultivates a praxis that seeks to emphasize the requirement of love in the service of justice.

The hallmark of Martin Luther King, Jr.'s prophetic ministry was the praxis of love inseparably linked with the demands of justice. King's leadership gave a new prophetic and theological perspective to the black church's social responsibility and ministry. To a large degree, the theology of the Civil Rights era served as a model for a new "prophetic theology" that underscored the role of the black church as a historically conscious liberation community. In linking up with black people's authentic struggles, recognizing black needs, arousing black aspirations, legitimizing black expectations, serving as the vanguard for black demands, King was able to raise the collective potential of the various arms of the black community, creating the atmosphere for the emergence of new organizations (SNCC, CORE, SCLC). During the King era, an alternative consciousness to the dominant culture was born. Black churches and the social hope of the black community were united with the freedom story of the black Christian tradition that revived liberation praxis in the church's ministry.

The political personalism of King's style of leadership, combined with prophetic radicalism, produced substantial social change but could not be sustained after his assassination. In the post-King era, leadership both in the Civil Rights organizations (SCLC, CORE, SNCC) and in the black church was not able to sustain the model of leadership King projected, which consists of "charismatic leadership under the rubric of

---

[49]Ibid., 8.
[50]Walter Brueggemann, *Prophetic Imagination,* 23.

political and prophetic fervor."[51] There was no well-developed collectivity of lay and clergy leaders left to continue the liberation strategies of the movement. James MacGregor Burns remarks:

> Political personalism is a promising strategy for dynamic, charismatic leadership; its great weakness for those interested in realizing political goals and achieving social change is that the movement rises and falls with the success of a less than immortal leader.[52]

After King's death, a crisis in leadership succession and continuity developed, leaving a vacuum for continuing the liberating praxis he inspired.

An action-reflection model for developing praxis skills in the black church is vital for prophetic understanding of a ministry committed to social justice. When the church does not give serious theological reflection to past prophetic actions, the locus of praxis for present and future actions is lost. The prophetic character of ministry in the black church suggests at least four perspectives that are essential for effective leadership in the praxis of liberation: (1) a reorientation of ministry that places emphasis on individualistic theodicies toward the quest for collective justice, (2) a theological orientation that encourages structural social changes, (3) a commitment to the importance of communal power that seeks to encourage a broader social milieu of the black community, and (4) a concept of the black church that would serve as agent of God's liberation in the world. These perspectives of prophetic ministry in the black church are essential if the church is to give leadership to the movement for social justice.

The Reformist Model

Black pastors have been politically involved on behalf of the black community from the inception of African American history. The political disenfranchisement of black people demanded that the black church and its leaders "mix politics and religion" and become actively engaged with the political liberation of black people. Black religious leaders have believed in the American democratic system and felt that if the principles

---

[51]Gayraud Wilmore, *Black Religion and Black Radicalism,* 174.
[52]James MacGregor Burns, *Leadership* (New York: Harper and Row, 1978) 267.

of justice espoused in the constitution were fully implemented, black people would live in freedom and justice.

Calling upon this nation to honor the demands for justice in the Constitution for all its citizens remains the central commitment of black religious leaders who seek political transformation of the black community. Black religious leaders have known that a major area of black victimization in the United States is a faulty political system that discriminates against people of color. The consistent history of uneven distribution of economic and material resources in the black community has forced black religious leaders to challenge politically the system toward social reform. Today, of the twenty-two million persons who need public assistance for food, a significant percentage are people of color and women. Political reformists among black religious leaders seek to transform a system that is creating a permanent underclass in America.

Adam Clayton Powell, who was pastor of the historic Abyssinian Baptist Church in New York's Harlem district and served as a U.S. congressman for twenty-two years, is a model of reformist political leadership in the black church tradition. Persons like former presidential contender Jesse Jackson, New York congressman Floyd Flake, and Washington D.C. congressman Walter E. Fauntroy represent the reformist tradition that was born in Reconstruction-era politics. The genius of Powell's reformist leadership was his theological perspective of political transformation for administering justice in the black community. Powell combined a prophetic theological orientation with political wisdom by involving the church significantly in the political, social, economic, and educational dimensions of black political empowerment.[53] As a charismatic leader, Powell successfully wedded the theology of the black church with pragmatic political concerns.

Poverty and the feminization of poverty, unemployment and rampant homelessness, environmental racism, privatization of education, and the debates regarding affirmative action versus quotas are grave political concerns that have inspired an increased interest in electoral politics among black religious leaders.

Reformists like Powell, Jackson, and Fauntroy believe that America's political system is redeemable even though the signs of political

---

[53]Ibid., 133.

deterioration and injustice point in the opposite direction. In the main, black religious leaders seek political office not only to seek political empowerment of the black community but to "redeem the soul of America" as well. Black religious leaders believe that the pervasiveness of racism in the structures of American government makes its difficult for the American political system to change gross inequalities and injustices in the black community. Even though passage of the 1965 Voter's Rights Act achieved optimistic figures in legislative government across the nation, the social crisis in poor and oppressed communities has become worse. The face of poverty in urban black communities remains as it was twenty-five years ago.

By using the black church as a power base, many black religious leaders have sought and won political office. But grass-roots political organizations see a greater role for the black church in the political empowerment of the black community. The creative and productive involvement of the black church in the political liberation of the black community is critical. There are several ways in which black pastors can serve as a positive political influence in the black community.[54]

First, the black pastor can establish a political action committee that establishes procedures for determining the qualifications of all political aspirants and makes recommendation to the congregation based on findings.[55]

Second, a seminar or study session on the political structures that govern the community's future should be a part of an ongoing assessment in the church's action in reflection. People should be informed on how the system works, what the issues are with special emphasis on how they impact upon the black community, and what their responsibilities and opportunities are. The black church is and should be a source for the education, training and development of political leadership.

Third, the political systems of local municipalities and our national government need monitoring by the church to determine how decisions

---

[54]Kelly Millers Smith, Sr., "Religion as a Force in Black America," 204-206. Smith believed that political transformation of the black community is the prophetic task of the black church.

[55]Ibid., 204.

being made will affect the black community.[56] The black church should serve as a community forum for ongoing dialogue regarding the political future and social transformation of the black community. It can play a major role in organizing the community for political action and social change. The church must serve as a base in the community for the creation of a social justice agenda. The church can present the agenda to political leaders and also lobby for its implementation in municipal, state, and national governments.

Finally, the black church must work with other groups and organizations as a collaborative/supportive agency.[57] This network of associations can include local and national political organizations; as well as such vital organizations as the NAACP, the Urban League, OIC; local ministerial and civic organizations; as well as national organizations such as the Congress of National Black Churches. As the moral agent and authority in the black community, the black church has the responsibility and challenge to rise up to the fullness of its potential in terms of influencing political and social reforms in this nation for the treatment of the poor and the oppressed.

Nationalistic Model

Unlike the reformist model of political leadership, black religious leaders who consider themselves in the black nationalistic tradition invest little or no hope in the future prospects for transformation of American politics on the behalf of blacks. Thus they believe that the black community has no hopeful existence in American society. Advocates of the black nationalistic tradition consider racial injustice inevitable as long as blacks are controlled by a dominant white society, and consequently they advocate some form of racial separation to allow blacks to gain a self-determined vision and control over their own destiny. Self-determination is the basic ethical and political principle underlying the thought and action of black religious leaders of the black nationalistic tradition.[58]

---

[56]Ibid., 205.
[57]Ibid.
[58]Ibid., 148.

Theologically and spiritually, the nationalistic contribution to liberation praxis in the black religious tradition is related to their concept of blackness. Prominent exponents of black nationalistic thought (such as Henry McNeal Turner, Marcus Garvey, Malcolm X, and Albert Cleage) affirm the importance of black consciousness, black unity, black self-love, and self-liberation in the black struggle for justice. Black nationalists have no difficulty in showing the relationship of biblical justice to the contemporary black situation because, in their view, the Old and New Testaments sanction the building of a black nation under the justice of God.

According to the black nationalist religious perspective, freedom, unity, love, and knowledge of blackness are interdependent elements in black people's struggle for liberation.[59] For example, nationalism as expressed in the views of Malcolm X sought to empower black self-respect through an appreciation and acceptance of blackness. As long as blacks are "culturally dead," alienated from their history and self-understanding, and separated from their black heritage they cannot create a black future of self-determination and freedom. As James Cone notes, Malcolm X viewed physical servitude as inseparably linked to the mental slavery of black people, which he described as a condition of seeing blackness as inferior and not as a badge of honor and divine worth. Malcolm X charged that black people do not know who they are in a white man's world: "We are a lost people, we don't know our name, language, homeland, God, or religion."[60]

While many traditional black pastors find aspects of black nationalism theologically unacceptable, one notes that many of them secretly admire the call of black nationalists for restoring dignity, self-determination, and self-respect to black people.[61] Malcolm's philosophy of black unity and wholeness is having greater ascendancy in black religious thought today, than it did when he was alive. Malcolm's class analysis and critique of race and religion in America cannot be easily dismissed

---

[59]James H. Cone, *Martin and Malcolm and America: A Dream or A Nightmare*, 105.
[60]Ibid., 105.

[61]In his landmark scholarship on the thought of Martin Luther King, Jr., and Malcolm X, Cone points out the extreme importance and value of Malcolm's race critique of Western Christianity for understanding the barriers to black liberation in America.

by those who take seriously the liberation of not only black people but the whole human race. The black nationalists' perspective of race pride, black peoplehood, and black self-determination offers an Afrocentric alternative for reversing the cultural, political, and social destruction of black heritage and life. The critique of race, ethnicity, and Western Christianity by black nationalists challenges the black church to reflect on the kind of theology and praxis that does justice to the legitimate grievances and contradictions of black existence in America.

Liberating praxis, as previously argued, underscores the need for a critique of what it means to be black and Christian. This critique calls for the theological particularization of blackness and the universalization of liberation as the purpose of God for oppressed peoples. As J. DeOtis Roberts notes, theological reflection on blackness must be particular but not provincial.[62] "We need to combine a concrete contextual orientation with a universal vision . . . it should lead to humanization for ourselves and the entire human family."[63] It is important that black Christians see and understand blackness as providential and destined for a special role in the economy of God. As the resident theologian in a church, the black pastor's theological and ethical task is to train black congregants to think theologically about blackness and God's salvific concern for the total liberation of God's entire creation.

Moral Leadership

The various perspectives and styles of black religious leaders call for moral leadership. Black pastors must keep their moral perspective of leadership clear and committed to the goal of liberation and social justice. Since the moral leadership of the black pastor is seen as the moral authority of the black community, the black community's quest for justice cannot be achieved without moral leadership. Moral leadership, in James MacGregor Burns' view, is leadership committed to social change. As Burns notes, moral leadership is authentic leadership committed to social justice change.[64] In some cases, black congregants are adversely

---

[62]J. DeOtis Roberts, *Black Theology in Dialogue,* 21.

[63]Ibid., 18.

[64]James MacGregor Burns, *Leadership* (New York: Harper and Row, 1978) 35.

affected by a male-oriented charisma and authoritarian leadership styles that encourage sexism and abuse of power, thereby reducing the capacity of churches to foster an inclusive, prophetic consciousness in the praxis of liberation. This expression of leadership encourages political passivity, exclusivism, accommodation, and resignation to the status quo; it is not moral leadership, because it denies the development of the full potential of black people.

The basic presupposition of Burns' definition of moral leadership is that leadership involves a relational dynamic between "the leader and the led" wherein mutual fulfillment—of fundamental values, needs, aspirations, expectations, and goals of both the leader and the led one—is met. In the case of the leader and the led in black churches, the values are centered in the need for power and the ability to act in public life in order to obtain a liberated future. Leadership in the black community is moral when it is seen as mutually collective, an inclusive and reciprocal process involving the collective purposes of the leader and the led in specific motives and values and various economic and political resources that are mutually held by both leaders and followers.[65] Burns understands moral leadership as interacting with transforming leadership (leadership committed to social transformation) and transactional leadership (exchange of loyalty for promises) models. The acid test of effective leadership is its moral commitment toward the realization of mutually held goals, effecting measurable change in the common life of the followers as well as leaders.[66]

The moral dimension of black religious leadership, as defined in this discussion, does not support a separation between social activism and Christian spirituality, private and public faith.[67] Black ministers remain divided regarding the issue of Christian spirituality and social activism. Many black pastors have slipped back into a progressively insulated approach to ministry. J. DeOtis Roberts accurately describes this pattern in these terms:

---

[65]Ibid., 51.

[66]Ibid., 417.

[67]Harold E. Quinley, *The Prophet Clergy: Social Activism and the Protestant Ministers* (New York: John Wiley and Sons, 1974) 20. Conflict that arose during the Martin Luther King, Jr., era between King and Joseph H. Jackson, former president of the National Baptist Convention, is an example of the polarization.

Emphasis is shifting from transforming or saving society to a state of soul or personal relationship with Christ. We have American spiritualism and the success syndrome. Churches are revitalized by speaking in tongues, by an outpouring of the gift of Spirit, by a rebirth of Pentecostalism. . . . Trust in our technological utopia has been shattered by a sense of emptiness. Protest against war and racism has fallen back on the individual experience of God, which has deep roots in American Christianity.[68]

We have argued that leadership is a collective process that seeks to mobilize the resources of people toward the fulfillment of the moral goals of black community.[69] A moral commitment to social change seeks to empower the black community for a self-determined future. Black religious leadership has been most effective in serving the collective purpose of black people when it has kept together spiritual awareness and social political activism.[70] By forging a vital unity between intellectual concerns, spirituality, and social transformation, black religious leadership gives moral vitality and relevance to the black church's liberation praxis.[71]

In conclusion, to meet the challenge of liberation ministry, black churches must readjust their models of leadership through a rereading of the black Christian tradition. The black pastor's role is to reawaken a prophetic social conscience that brings with it the potential for self-liberation of congregations in the black community. New challenges of cultural and racial pluralism in the black community require the black church to rethink the official structures of ministry and leadership. The restructuring of ministry must include addressing the external and internal forms of race and gender exploitation and class oppression.[72] To serve the collective purpose of the black community, black pastors "must struggle

---

[68]J. DeOtis Roberts, *A Black Political Theology* (Philadelphia: The Westminster Press, 1974) 25.

[69]Burns, *Leadership,* 460.

[70]Archie Smith, Jr., "The Relational Self in the Black Church: From Bondage to Challenge" in *Changing Views of the Human Condition,* ed. Paul W. Pruyser (Macon, GA: Mercer University Press, 1987) 136-53.

[71]*Lewis V. Baldwin, There is a Balm in Gilead: The Cultural Roots of Martin Luther King, Jr.,* (Minneapolis: Fortress Press, 1991) 227.

[72]Smith, "The Relational Self in the Black Church," 146.

against sexism within their own structures."[73] The black church's traditional structures for authorizing leadership must be carefully examined to
determine if these structures support the moral demands of justice and a
theology of a shared liberating praxis. Leadership structures in the black
church must be revised to foster inclusive, collaborative and shared
models of ministry.

Wedding theological vision, social praxis, and liberation strategies
with Christian spirituality will require black pastors to be open to public
critique by those with whom they share ministry and to be held
accountable for social actions. The exclusive model of "one-man rule"
leadership perfected through the charismatic gifts of the black preacher
is not sufficient for achieving the end-goal of the reign of God. Whereas,
dependence on a charismatic model of leadership leads to unaccountable
power and unaccountable action. A major task of black religious leadership is to facilitate a process of equipping those who comprise the black
churches with praxis skills for reflecting theological on social ministry.
Black church leadership must keep the communal and collective qualities
of the black Christian tradition alive, and they must engage black
Christians in theological reflection on the black church's story and
ministry tradition.

Black Religious Leadership and Communal Power

Liberating leadership in the black churches requires a cultivation of
communal power. Many churches experience failure in their social ministry programs for a number of reasons—but mainly because of the lack
of shared communal power. For our purposes, power is defined as the
ability to act on the behalf of one's self-interest. Communal power is the
ability to act on behalf of building and sustaining relationships in
community. Communal power is the capacity both to produce collective
consciousness (affect) and to undergo change (effect).[74] Communal power
is a force that recognizes the potentiality for "genuine community."[75]
Ministry, as we have discussed it, is a mutual process grounded in

---

[73]Ibid., 143.
[74]Peter J. Paris, *Social Teachings of the Black Churches,* 118.
[75]Ibid., 417.

relationality toward the end of accomplishing social transformation; it is ultimately committed to the building of community. Black pastors who are committed to this type of social ministry must be willing to share power within the institutional life and culture of the black church. Communal power is relational in character. In its relational quality, communal power cares for the total being of others; it is committed to empowering others to act.

Further, unilateral power is the opposite of communal or shared power. Extreme use of unilateral power by black pastors or other leaders within the churches who have molded a power base for their self-interest severely hinders a process of ministry based on relationality. An inappropriate use of unilateral power works in opposition to shared ministry and cooperation in liberation praxis.[76] The fact that many black pastors are unequivocally committed to the use of unilateral power is the primary cause for many and varied conflicts in the internal life of black churches. Abuse of power by black church leaders is responsible for much fragmentation of ministry initiatives.

Unilateral power is interested only in its own purposes and reduces persons to means to its own ends. Unilateral power commits the pastor to a decision-making process that maintains control of people and their aspirations for ministry. It is an exercise of *power over* rather than a sharing of *power with people* in the congregation.[77] Floyd Massey, Jr., and Samuel McKinney in their book, *Church Administration in the Black Perspective*, identify the possible ramifications of this ecclesial problem in the black church:

> Most administration in black churches seems to be run by the grace of God and the mercy of the people, without adequate records, permanent paid employees. . . . (The black church has lost many members on the basis that we never use them in the church structure unless they can be used for the personal benefit of the minister and his [her] administration.[78]

---

[76]Ibid., 114.

[77]Paulo Freire, *Pedagogy of the Oppressed*, 29.

[78]Floyd Massey, Jr., and Samuel McKinney, *Church Administration in the Black Church Perspective* (Valley Forge: Judson Press, 1976) 11.

Because many black church members are captives of the charismatic appeal of black pastors and are conditioned to being acted upon by unilateral power decisions, they are handicapped in understanding how they might share in the liberation the community desperately needs and the liberation they seek for themselves. Black churches that exist in an atmosphere where unilateral power is abused inevitably contribute to the emotional estrangement among their members that destroys love and the capacity to do justice.[79]

In contrast to unilateral power, communal power is open to a collective leadership style. The sharing of power is the key to collective leadership. Collective leadership is accountable to the larger judgment of a group; it deepens the investment of ownership of the church's vision for social transformation. One of the most serious problems facing the black church today may be the isolation of black pastors from his/her solidarity with the laity. This contact would allow for mutuality and the developing of a bond in Christian social ministry. A ministry process that is built upon relationships within a congregation enables a church to discover what life values connect its members in Christian ministry.

Leaders who share in communal expressions of power can bring about something compatible with their self-interest and the hopes and aspirations of the group. Leadership that inspires effective joint action has the capacity to be influenced by the group; it learns from the group and the changes the group's joint actions accomplish.[80] The goal of building community is best served when members of a church become co-creators of their history and work collectively for the accomplishment of a liberated future.

Communal power, on the other hand, is committed to the development of human beings. It seeks to enable them to act or participate in the vision of community. When people exist in an atmosphere where power is relational, they more freely share one another's stories of pain, joy, success, and failure. Black people's daily existence in a world of racial and social oppression creates the opportunity for the sharing of numerous stories that draw people together in relationship and release power in the group to act in liberating ways. As the black community—and the world around it—has become more diverse in self-interests and more socially

---

[79]Peter J. Paris, *Social Teaching Teachings of the Black Churches,* 114.
[80]Ibid., 118.

stratified, the cultivation of communal power will be essential for the black church if it is to maintain relevant contact with the liberation needs of black people.

Social Stratification and Class Consciousness

Black pastors today have the difficult task of connecting and holding together a socially stratified black constituency. The black pastor's charisma alone is insufficient to appeal to the diversity of self-interests present in a local congregation created by the prosperity of a few and the economic disadvantage of many in and around the church. Statistical economic reports indicate considerable change has occurred during the past two decades that divides the black middle class from those reported by Julius Wilson as "the truly disadvantaged."[81] Unfortunately, economic diversity has impoverished a black Christian spirituality in solidarity with liberating praxis. Howard Dodson explains:

> The identification of black liberation with the material success of a few, physically and mentally severed from the black masses, makes mockery of the unity essential for the salvation of us all. Even the material good fortune of that few are poisoned by emptiness and isolation from the people's struggle without which the mission of Jesus Christ can be neither understood nor undertaken.[82]

Dodson further states:

> Today, black Americans and black churches are at a moral crossroad, situated somewhere between their historic past and the elusive goal of full justice and freedom. They proceed toward the twenty-first century more diversified and less unified on their objectives and less certain about a common role in creating a new society.[83]

---

[81]Julius Wilson, *The Truly Disadvantaged: The Inner City, The Underclass, and Public Policy* (Chicago: University of Chicago Press, 1987) chap. 2.

[82]Howard Dodson, "Review to Review," *The Witness.* (March, 1978): 8-13.

[83]Ibid., 8.

Though social stratification has created camps of class consciousness in black churches, it presents the black pastor and church at large with the opportunity to discover that which makes the black church what it is as well as its historic and contemporary reason for existing. This opportunity will not be met nor welcomed by black church leaders trapped in a narrow provincialism and one-dimensional understanding of leadership and Christian ministry. Nor will relevant changes occur through spirited preaching, extemporaneous prayer, pious sentimentalism, individualistic hymns, literalism in biblical interpretation, heightened emotionalism, materialism confused with Christian authentication, and emphasis on conventional morality based on heaven or hell choices of salvation.[84] Rather, the challenge of this opportunity calls for taking the sharing of communal power seriously, inviting people to reconnect themselves, and bringing the church to a new life orientation through reflection on and commitment to the black Christian tradition. Gayraud Wilmore asserts, "The black Christian tradition that nurtured and the culture that enriched the black church's past will evaporate into the aridity of a crassly materialistic middle-classism" if black church leaders do not cultivate forms of liberation discipleship in local congregations.[85] As previously noted, the core content of this reflection asks:

> How can black Christians use the history, culture, and experience of their historic struggle for freedom to enhance the proclamation of the gospel of Jesus Christ and the manifestation of Christ's power to transform not only Black humanity but the whole human race.[86]

Dodson, of The Black Theology Project, describes well the task this opportunity of ministry presents to the black churches:

> The task of creating the new society . . . will require that Blacks be willing to struggle, first, against the enemy within ourselves, our own individualism and our own political irresponsibility, our own victim mentality and our own reluctance to live up to our fullest potential as human beings—allowing us willingly to accept rather than avoid the

---

[84]Gayraud Wilmore, *Black and Presbyterian*, 63.
[85]Ibid., 113.
[86]Ibid., 84.

challenge and historic necessity to transform American society for the mutual benefit of everyone.[87]

Ministry in the black church is an attempt to preach, teach, and live out the biblical message of freedom under God in such ways that it reaches the realities of black existence in a context of cultural, social, political, and economic oppression. It is incumbent upon the black pastors and church leaders to invite theological reflection upon its social ministry from the perspective of the black Christian tradition and to discover a shared vision of liberation ministry.

Black Religious Leadership and Liberation Praxis

The role of black pastors in liberation praxis has four basic foci: (1) affirming black humanity under the grace of God, (2) functioning as a prophet, (3) giving guidance to the organization of the church's liberation efforts, and (4) interpreting the theological life of the congregation in the world. As previously stated, liberation praxis has an inner and outer meaning for the development of black Christian spirituality. Outwardly, it means exercising the power to throw off the economic, political, and ideological yoke of oppression. Inwardly, liberation means freedom from the internalization of oppression to arrive at a proper sense of self and right relation with God and the world. Persons are not sustained in liberation praxis by only crusading for social change, but through continuous events of "inward liberation" and reflection on ministry. "Inward liberation" is not only a prerequisite for social transformation, it preserves the revolutionary sense of purpose after social action and transformation.[88] The black pastor's role in the church is liberating praxis to facilitate the reflection that provides the bridge connecting action with vision. The black Christian tradition, black theological resources, and the lived experience of participants in ministry are accessible for this reflection and must be skillfully used by black pastors and lay leaders in group reflection.

---

[87]Archie Smith, Jr., *The Relational Self,* 13.
[88]Luther Smith, *The Prophetic As Mystic,* 173.

As previously discussed, praxis is reflection on ministry action; it is a mutual evaluative interaction that permits people to achieve a vision of community that could not be realized apart from shared reflection. That which is born in reflection grows to maturity and is completed in prophetic consciousness and action.[89]

In conclusion, the liberation struggle of the 1960s and the new social milieu of the 1980s and 1990s suggest a new agenda for the black church's social ministry. Ministry for social crisis calls for the church to engage in a process of interpretation and formation of its shared life and thought in ways that express the vitality of the black Christian tradition and lead to transformation of the world. The mission of the black church consists of a shared praxis ministry that is committed to the total liberation of God's entire creation.

---

[89]Howard Thurman, "Mysticism and Social Change," *Eden Theological Seminary Bulletin* 4 (Spring 1939): 11.

Appendix

A Call to a National Dialogue: The Challenge of a Black Theology to the African American Church[1]

I call heaven and earth to witness against you today that I have set before you life and death, blessings and curses. Choose life so that you and your descendants may live. (Deut 30:19 NRSV)

I. A Critical Choice

The African American Church is in crisis. A crisis that calls for a national dialogue. At a time in history when we are about to enter a new millennium, the African American Church stands at the crossroads of decision. Its traditional role as the conservator of Black culture and the conscience of the Black community is at stake. It must choose either life or death, blessings or curses. Whatever choice it makes will determine whether or not we and our descendants will live as a redeemed and redeeming community in this land where God has befriended us.

The signs of the crisis we face today are unmistakable:

---

[1]This working paper was used as the basis for A Call to a National Dialogue and Reflection on "What Does it Mean to be Black and Christian?" prepared by the Kelly Miller Smith Institute on African American Church Studies at the Divinity School of Vanderbilt University, Nashville, Tennessee, October 1992. The Dialogue was funded through grants from the Lilly Endowment, the PEW Charitable Trusts, and the Booth Ferris Foundation. Contributors included: Michael Battle, Hampton University, Hampton, VA; Elizabeth K. Burgess, Pleasant Green Baptist Church, Nashville, TN; Karen Y. Collier, Seay-Hubbard United Methodist Church, Nashville, TN; Bettye Collier-Thomas, Temple University, Philadelphia, PA; James H. Cone, Union Theological Seminary, New York, NY; Roscoe Cooper, Fifth Street Baptist Church, Richmond, VA; Odell McGlothian, American Baptist College, Nashville, TN; Samuel Proctor, United Theological Seminary, Dayton, OH; Alan Ragland, Memphis Theological Seminary, Memphis, TN; Gayraud Wilmore, Interdenominational Theological Center, Atlanta, GA; Prathia Hall-Wynn, United Theological Seminary, Dayton, OH; Forrest E. Harris, Sr., Kelly Miller Smith Institute, Nashville, TN; and Donna E. Allen, Vanderbilt University.

Witness—the social and economic descent of more than a third of the Black population into a burgeoning and permanent underclass.

Witness—the children of our impoverished, drug-infested neighborhoods coming to the point of birth, and yet dying in the womb of human possibility.

Witness—the rate of incarceration of young Black males that has 23 percent of those aged 20 to 29—almost one of every four—in prison, on bail, on probation or parole.[2]

Witness—the turning of thousands of our young people toward illegal drugs in a vain, hedonistic escape from reality, or an attempt to enter a degrading, criminal career.

Witness—the unprecedented assault on Black family life by urban violence, poverty, homelessness, and teenage pregnancy on the one hand, and on the other, the demands of an upwardly mobile, materialistic lifestyle that is scornful of God and has no place for the church of Jesus Christ.

Witness—the reversals in the public arena of hard won policies ensuring affirmative action for minorities and women.

Witness—the rampant individualism, the loss of community, and the decline of the Black Church as an effective agent for justice and liberation among all poor and oppressed people. The list goes on.

II. A Spiritual Crisis

The crisis that we are faced with does not simply reflect a crisis of social, economic, and political proportions, but also and more profoundly, a crisis of Black faith. As a people, we are losing the ability to hear God speaking to us in self-affirming and liberating ways. Hopelessness and despair have taken the place of faith for millions. For this reason, it is clear that what we are facing is essentially a *religious* crisis—a crisis of the Black Church in its historic role as the custodian of our values, and the moral arbiter and mentor of the African American community—both the churched and unchurched.

---

[2]See *The State of Black America, 1991*, ed. Janet Dewart (New York: The National Urban League, 1991).

All institutions in which we predominate, particularly our schools, colleges, seminaries and churches, are touched by this religious and moral crisis—this crisis of the Black spirit. As our ancestors heard and responded to God's call "to come and let us reason together" (Isa 1:18), we too need to come together today in order to clarify and articulate truths relative to this crisis. The word *crisis* not only points to the impending danger in which we stand, but also challenges us to reassess our situation as a people and a church and to seize the opportunity for a faithful response to God.

III. A Call to a National Dialogue

The purpose of this document is to summon our people to a national dialogue. A dialogue between pastors and theological professors, clergy, and laity, brothers and sisters—to articulate the broad outlines of *What it means to be both Black and Christian and to maintain, at one and the same time, both the unifying integrity of liberated individuals, and the rich diversity of a reconciled community of faith.* We speak, in this working paper, of a Black theology—a Black perspective on the faith of Jesus Christ and the faith of our ancestors—that will help us to straighten out the confusion in our minds, and that will clarify our purposes and goals as Black Christians.

If the ominous trends of oppression are to be turned back and the collapse of churches as agents of Black solidarity and liberation is to be reversed, then scholars of the academy and pastors of churches, denominational and congregational officials, professionals, students, artists, clergy, laity, women, and men must seriously engage in a protracted dialogue on the *nature of our dilemma, the means by which we can be extricated from it, and the reason for the hope that is in us* (see 1 Pet 3:15).

IV. Life or Death?

We have come to a moment in the 373 years of our pilgrimage in North America when we must make a decisive choice for life or death. Death means turning our backs on our historic identity as an African people transplanted on this soil by sinful people, but by God's good purpose (see Gen 50:19-20), to help the United States realize the full measure of its potential. Death means turning our backs on our perennial struggle for justice and equality. Death means turning our backs on the God who delivers the oppressed. Life, on the other hand, means affirming and celebrating the spiritual inheritance passed down to us from a kidnapped, tortured, and enslaved people who were determined *to be* and *to become* in spite of every attempt to dehumanize them. Life means choosing the God of our foreparents who has brought us thus far to be witnesses to the divine purpose of the redemption of all creation through struggle and hope (see Rom 8:19-25).

V. We Begin By Confessing Our Sins

As pastors and seminary professors, clergy and laity, women and men of the Christian faith, we confess our personal sins and the sins of the churches and educational institutions we serve.

We have not—loved God or our neighbors as we ought. We have been bloated with our own conceit, blind to the needs of the Samaritan lying by the side of the road, and corrupted by our desire for power, fame, and personal gain.

We have not—taken care of the household of God, like good stewards. Rather we have used it to prey on our people's emotions or their intellectual pride and gullibility. Instead of making the Black Church a missionary outpost and the Black school a beachhead in enemy territory, we have made them safe havens for the fearful, complacent, and snobbish.

We have not—spoken the truth in love or taken pains to study and prepare our own minds for teaching and leading in the complex world in which we live today.

We have not—accepted all people as children of God, whether good or bad, educated or uneducated, female or male, but we have been respecters of persons, preferring those who flatter and reward us.

We have not—stayed on the battlefield to fight until the war is over; instead, we have abandoned the struggle to secular institutions, and have made the Black Church subservient of conservative politicians and socially indifferent personalities who call themselves evangelists.

We confess that we are profoundly ashamed of all wherein we have displeased and dishonored God. All the ways in which we have trivialized the Church and corrupted the Academy. In this unprecedented crisis of our congregations, schools, and communities, we throw ourselves upon the mercy of God, pleading that through this act of public confession we may prove ourselves sincerely repentant and through this proposal for national dialogue, worthy of giving leadership to a new life together.

VI. We Receive the Assurance of Pardon

The Scripture tells us that, "If we confess our sins, God is faithful and just, and will forgive our sins and cleanse us from all unrighteousness" (1 John 1:9 NRSV). We accept this assurance of pardon with joy and declare it for ourselves and all our brothers and sisters, within and outside of the Church.

We celebrate the fact that despite all our shortcomings we are forgiven people; that because of God's grace the Black church, the Black family, and the Black school are still alive, vibrant, and girded, with strength for dealing with this portentous crisis. We who have the courage to admit the painful truth—that we have often been greater enemies to ourselves than our oppressors, call all African Americans to confession of our sins and to the assurance that the blood of Christ redeems us from the curse of the law, which is our just condemnation.

Crisis suggests both negative and positive possibilities. We do not assume that nothing good is happening in the Black Church. **We believe, that many are being blessed because of foundational Black institutions; that Black theology is already being practiced in many places by thousands of unacclaimed pastors, teachers, lay leaders; and that obedience and faithfulness are normative virtues in many of our communities today.** We thank God that the Black Church has stood for social transformation with a profound belief that "everybody talkin' bout heaven ain't goin' there;" that the gospel must be *lived out* in the tension between sociology and theology, between the public arena and the sanctuary.

The sociology of the Black Church is expressed in theological terms and the theology of the Black Church is expressed in sociological terms. Because of this tradition of theological realism the Black Church has always understood with crystal clarity what Jesus meant when he said:

> For I was hungry and you gave me food, I was thirsty and you gave me drink, I was a stranger and you welcomed me, I was naked and you clothed me, I was sick and you visited me, I was in prison and you came to me. (Matt 25:35-36 NRSV)

In fact, the supreme paradox of our situation is that despite the tragic overtones of our crisis, we can come together for study and dialogue in praise and thanksgiving to the God who has been so good to us. Despite our weaknesses and failures, despite all that we have endured in the past or will be called upon to suffer in the future, we can still say with the Psalmist:

> Lord, thou hast been our dwelling place in all generations. Before the mountains were brought forth, or ever thou hast formed the earth and the world, even from everlasting to everlasting, thou art God. (Ps 90:1-2 NRSV)

VII. What is Theology and What Does It Have To Do With Us?

Theology is the process of reflecting upon God's involvement in human life. Although an academic discipline, it is also the way any person appropriates the faith. In a real sense, all of us are theologians, for theology is the only way that reason and faith embrace each other. Every Christian is a theologian! It is our duty, as faithful believers, to do theology!

To do theology means to make an effort to understand, declare, and live out who God is, what God demands, and what God has done and is doing now for our salvation. Then, in the light of that *theology*, that is, the knowledge of ourselves, God, and the world, we must respond in faith, love, and obedience. *Theology in this sense is the work of the whole Church and the individual members of every congregation.* Without question, preaching is one of the mightiest tools the Black Church has for expressing our theology.

In the Black Church, the preaching moment is an opportunity to present a knowledge of ourselves and of God. The Black Church has long recognized the central role of preaching in the faithful presentation and doing of a relevant theology. One Black theologian put it this way:

It is the unenviable task of preachers to wrestle honestly with the word of God, to experience its critical power, for themselves and for the people they preach to—but always within the situation and the experience of their people, so that the preachers will be understandable and relevant. . . . It is preaching that addresses their deepest existential problems, preaching that speaks to the whole of their existence. For Blacks this means that the preacher must address not merely their being in the world, but their being Black in the world.[3]

No one can do theology in a cultural vacuum. No one can respond to God outside of his or her existential context. We do not meet God as disembodied spirits, but in our flesh and blood, and as *physical, historical creatures in concrete, living situations*. This means that there is no absolutely unconditioned universal theology. Even the New Testament was written in Greek and reflects the character, mind-set, and situation of Greek-speaking people in Asia Minor during the first two centuries of the Christian era. Theology is bound to time, to culture, and to experience. Although we know God as individuals *all* theology is influenced by and reflects—in one way or another—the historical and experiential circumstances of a people, a nation, or a neighborhood. God comes to us and we respond to God where we are placed in the world. We can do no more nor less than apprehend and respond to God out of the content of our social situation and experience.

VIII. What is Black Theology?

Black theology is Story. It is the story of our tedious pilgrimage as daughters and sons of Africa in North America. It is the story of how we have scaled mountains that seemed unclimbable and made our way through valleys that have been a veritable low ground of sorrow.

Black theology is the story of our faith in God. The God who hears bondage groans and comes to deliver the oppressed; who causes them to become agents of their own salvation. Black theology is the story of our journey with Jesus Christ, our Savior, and Liberator.

---

[3]Allan Boesak, *The Finger of God* (New York: Orbis Books, 1982) 7-8.

Black theology is the story of our faith-understanding and our freedom struggle. It is the story of how our faith functioned as the cornerstone of our movement toward freedom.

Our faith has inspired, fueled, and fired our freedom struggle and enabled us to overcome extraordinary hardship and hurdles from the early days of our captivity until now.

Black theology is biblical. It is the recital of the story of Joseph who reminds us of Frederick Douglass, Harriet Tubman and other great abolitionists who refused to abandon the enslaved in a strange land. It tells the story of Esther who did not glory in the fact that she had become royalty, but heard the cries of her people. It tells the story of the three Hebrew boys who would rather choose death than forsake the God of their weary years and silent tears.

Black theology is contextual. Black theology interprets the Bible in the context of Black life because our questions and answers have not been, and cannot be articulated by others as fully and accurately as by ourselves. Black theology, by necessity, comes out of the context of Black life. It makes no claims for absoluteness, nor pretends unanimity. Not all Black Christians affirm the same faith. But we begin the national dialogue believing that those Black Christians who affirm that liberation from every form of oppression is at the heart of the gospel; that Jesus Christ is the Liberator; and that there can be no true knowledge of the God of the Bible without resistance to injustice and oppression of every kind will also affirm the legitimacy of a Black theology. We may say, therefore, that Black theology is story that is primarily biblically based, and secondly, rigorously contextual.

At a time when others make predictions about the future of our community and paint a gloomy picture of the extinction of African American people as a distinct entity, we need Black theology. We need it because we must claim not only the faith of our mothers and fathers, but understand what we are up against today and the work we must do to claim our future. We need Black theology because many Black adults and children are being swept up by conservative White evangelical congregations and television ministries that speak of a "colorless gospel" that overlooks the age-old problems of race, class, and gender oppression. We need Black theology because some brands of White theology are being used to effectively brainwash our people. We need Black theology because it tells *our* story, and no one, not even the most trustworthy, and paternalistic White televangelist, can tell our story for us.

We must tell our story in the church School, the Sabbath School, and in the classrooms and clubrooms of our communities. We must tell it in video and film. We must tell it in pamphlets, denominational literature, magazines, and scholarly books. We must tell our story in denominational gatherings, in ecumenical ministerial alliances, in local, regional, and national dialogue sessions. *We must tell the story of what it means to be Black and Christian in America today. That story will inspire us and our children. It will inform us, and illuminate what God requires of us for the living of these days as God's African American people. Thus, we turn to the central question of our dialogue.*

IX. What Does It Mean To Be Black and Christian?

It is not possible to be a Black Christian, in the sense in which we are using those terms in this working paper, without recognizing the deep ambiguity and paradox that are at the conjunction of these two ways of being. Malcolm X described Christianity as the "perfect slave religion" because he saw how White people invented a religion calculated to keep Black people passive in slavery and subservient after emancipation. Therefore, the first requirement for understanding what it means to be Black and Christian is to admit that Christianity has been used to subjugate Africans and African Americans. Too many of us lack the spiritual and intellectual courage to make that admission. But only after we have made it can we begin to see how Blackness, as a state of mind, as a hermeneutical suspicion, and as a theological and cultural demystification of Anglo-Saxon religion and culture, can correct the distortions that modern racism induced into the message and mission of Jesus.

To be *Black* means many things. It means to accept Africa as the place of one's cultural and religious roots. It means to be identified with the rich heritage left by African men, women, and children who were forcibly brought to this land and whose history is replete with stories of great empires, powerful queens and kings, and a way of life that traditionally appreciated the whole of creation and recognized a profound spiritual reality within and behind the artifactual universe. Being Black is to be immersed in a humanistic and pragmatic culture transmitted through a strong oral tradition of storytelling, proverbs, songs, music, dance, and sculpture.

In racist societies Blackness has carried a negative connotation. White has been defined as good and Black as bad. *Webster's Third New International Dictionary* gives the following character definitions under the words White and Black.

> **White**: "free from blemish, moral strain or impurity; outstandingly righteous; innocent; not marked by malignant influence; notably pleasing as auspicious; fortunate; notably ardent; decent; in a fair and uprightly manner; a sterling man."

> **Black**: "outrageously wicked, a villain; dishonorable; expressing or indicating disgrace, discredit or guilt; connected with the devil; expressing menace; sullen; hostile; unqualified; committing a violation of public regulation; illicit, illegal; affected by some undesirable condition."

With these definitions is it surprising that, even though he was not European, Jesus in both White and Black churches is imaged as a blond, blue-eyed, White man? It should be obvious why it is necessary to incorporate a race critique into our understanding of the gospel. How can the Black Church proclaim a liberating gospel and ignore the cultural and theological bondage of African American Christians to Euro-American myths and values? To be Black means to imagine, think, and create out of an Afrocentricity accepted by God as the vehicle of revelation and redemption (see Acts 2:7-11).

To be *Christian* also means many things. It means, first, to be a follower, a disciple of Jesus of Nazareth; a believer in his Lordship and Messianic vocation. Like being Black, being Christian is clouded in many complexities and ambiguities. Just as there are Blacks who are self-esteeming and self-denigrating, enthusiastic and apathetic, loyal and disloyal, there are Christians who exhibit the same strengths and weaknesses. In the final analysis, to be authentically Christian must mean that one strives to walk in the way of Jesus and, in some measure, accepts Jesus Christ as Lord and savior.

When we put together these two ways of being—being Black and being Christian—we have a unique combination of histories, cultural images and perspectives, moral visions, and commitments which Black religious thinkers—from Robert Alexander Young and David Walker to James H. Cone and Prathia Hall Wynn—have labored to spell out in terms of specific choices and decisions in specific times and places. *What it means to be Black and Christian cannot be static or carved in stone, rather, out of necessity it must change over time. It is dynamic and responsive to the movement of God through history and open to the winds of the Holy Spirit.* Blackness and the Christian faith are so often misunderstood, as a result of being placed too strictly in opposition to each other, or trivialized by being too easily reconciled and reduced to a premature and conventional sameness. This is precisely why dialogue and debate are urgently necessary today.

If Black theology is story, then to be Black and Christian means to pantomime that story—to act it out on the stage of one's own life; to participate in the message and meaning of that story in proclamation and demonstration, alongside sisters and brothers who see themselves as actors in the same story. Across the United States today hundreds, perhaps thousands, of African American congregations are demonstrating that it is possible to integrate their Blackness and their faith in a way that not only bestows wholeness and healing upon individuals and families, but also engages communities in corporate ministries of intervention and transformation of the structures of social, economic, and political life.

We propose for the national dialogue the thesis that: Being Black and Christian is an individual, family, and congregational lifestyle that reflects our acceptance of our African origins, our inseverable ties to our slave ancestors, and our identification with the millions of excluded Black people who continue to sink in the quagmire of racism, sexism, and poverty. To be Black and Christian gives the mission of the Realm of God a special configuration and character, creating a unique religious symbolism and liturgical expression, and a distinctive spirituality and worship that are characteristics of our historic peoplehood.

X. God's Special Challenge to the Black Church Today
Becoming Sisters and Brothers in the Same Struggle

We cannot conclude this discussion without acknowledging that one of the most disturbing aspects of the crisis in the contemporary Black Church and community is the Black Church's historical ambivalence toward women in the Church. African American churches have, in large measure, adopted the patriarchal attitudes of White Christians regarding women. To the extent that our churches have accepted the patriarchal doctrines and practices of White Christianity we are faced today with a Black religious dilemma that has critical implications for our liberation struggle. The issue is larger than women in ministry. *The issue is the Church and Women.* We desperately need a Black theological and social analysis to help us clarify this aspect of the crisis, lest the Black Church become a stumbling block to its own mission of salvation and liberation.

Sexism in the Church represents a theological scandal. It exalts the genital fixations and sexual distortions of the culture to the level of a false theology and dares to blame that bigotry on God. Everything we know about God tells us clearly that the living God is not a bigot. Sexism, like racism, is idolatry. The scandal is even more outrageous when we who have been victims of the idolatry of racism, and know its abuse, stoop to practice the kindred idolatry of sexism. Careful examination of every biblical text commonly used to deny the equality and the ministry of women in Church and society will liberate Black Christians from misinterpretations that dishonor the character of the Creator and of humankind.

We are called to confront not only the theological scandal of sexism, but also the sociological crisis it precipitates in our communities. African Americans have historically understood our survival and freedom to be dependent upon our togetherness. Some of us are attempting today to deny that sexism is a problem in the Black community, to do so is to ignore the struggle of our sisters. Any authentic dialogue between Black women and men will reveal that sexism is a problem; real, pervasive, and destructive to our individual and collective existence.

Sexism not only limits the development and progress of African American women, it also undermines and retards the progress of African American people as a whole. The struggle for liberation will not move forward without the full participation and contribution of African American women. The incomes of African American women have always been critical to the survival and well being of our families. Whether or not we admit it, Black women have always been at the heart of our struggle. The continued active commitment, participation, and leadership of Black women is critical. The model of leadership and followership which we must leave for our children who must go into the twenty-first century must be one of full partnership among sisters and brothers united in one struggle in the name of Christ.

Unfortunately, many destructive myths are being circulated about us and believed by us. The notion that the "over-achievement" of Black women has retarded the progress of Black men has been one of the most devastating. This false allegation is promoting the break-up of families and turning us against ourselves by making Black women scapegoats and permitting the real culprit, a racist, sexist, White society, to remain unchallenged. We can not afford to be immobilized by attacks on each other. Being Black and Christian means, among other things, that our collective memories of our mothers and grandmothers and our unbiased observation of the contribution contemporary Black women are making, will not permit us to acquiesce in the lie that our Black sisters are the enemy. Black theology with its emphasis upon social analysis and praxis can liberate us from the counterproductive and destructive nature of sexism.

XI. Black Theology As Praxis

The brief congregational profiles below are examples of what being Black and Christian looks like in various settings. They are neither comprehensive nor exhaustive of what God is doing in the Black Church. Nor are they presented as models which must be duplicated in all congregations and communities. We present them as highly selective, but noteworthy examples of being Black and Christian in the world and, therefore, pointers in the direction of how Black theology is actually formulated and practiced in the United States today. These are only a few congregations of various denominations and in various parts of the nation that are examples of Black theology as *praxis*. Many more need to be identified and studied in the course of the national dialogue on what it means to be Black and Christian. The churches are listed in alphabetical order according to the name of the church.

Allen Temple Baptist Church, Oakland, California
Dr. J. Alfred Smith, Sr., Pastor

Allen Temple is concerned about ministry to the whole person, and has implemented a wide range of outreach ministries. Ministries in the area of education include: Hi-Rise Tutorial Program for elementary and secondary school students; Interface Institute, which assists junior and senior high school students in college preparatory math, science, and computer science; Highland Elementary School Network, which provides support services and educational enrichment for children in the neighborhood; adult education and community college in conjunction with the Oakland Unified School District and the Peralta Community College District; and The Business and Professional Women's Society which raises an average of $50,000 a year for scholarships. Social Services include: food programs; housing assistance; clothes pantry; and Job Services Committee, which provides job readiness seminars and employment services. Allen Temple works in partnership with Shiloh Christian Fellowship to support Star Shelter, a 30-bed facility for the homeless. Allen Temple has a AIDS Ministry Task Force, Oakland Crack Task Force, Boy Scout and Cub Scout programs; One Church One Child Program; and The Allen Temple Arms I and II apartment complexes, which provide housing for senior citizens and handicapped persons. The prison ministry of Allen Temple provides visitations; worship services; counseling; Bible study; and a Re-entry Program that assists parolees with employment, housing, education, and other re-entry needs. The Allen Temple Credit Union has over one million dollars in assets and provides loans and a wide range of financial services. Other ministries include: Senior Citizens Brown Bag, Sierra Leone Mission Project, Black Women's Support Group, Grief Counseling, and Cancer Support Group. Currently the church is in the midst of a campaign to raise 5-8 million dollars for a Family Life Center that will include 30-40 classrooms, a gymnasium, recreational facilities, a nursery, and office space.

Mariners' Temple Baptist Church, New York, New York
Rev. Dr. Suzan D. Johnson-Cook, Pastor

This congregation's ministry is divided into three major areas; worship, fellowship, and community outreach. The worship experience is diverse and consist of two major services—Sunday morning church, and a Wednesday Lunch Hour of Power that attracts some 500 participants from the business and professional community. The fellowship ministry is diverse and features an emphasis on education. There are Wednesday Services in Church and Teaching. A thematic approach to Bible study allows participants to choose specific areas of interest over a six to seven week period. Survival Kit helps people who are new to the faith make the transition to a new style of life particularly targeted to the young adult community. Sunday Afternoon Youth Alive provides young people, seven through twelve years of age, with recreational activities, workshops, Bible study, and creative ministries that build self-esteem, trust, and discipleship. The Thursday Noon Educational Service is a multiracial, multiethnic, and multiclass lunch hour Bible study that ministers to a variety of persons, including the unemployed, senior citizens, students, and professionals. The Afrocentric focus of ministry at Mariners' Temple is expressed in preaching, teaching, and Bible study. Thus, there is a study of the Black Presence in the Bible, a Multiethnic Learning Center with an after-school program designed to be inclusive of the Asian American, African American, Latin American and other ethnic groups in the community surrounding the church. Finally, there is a prison ministry, a Home for Developmentally Disabled Persons, and an Elders Care Program that reaches out to senior adults.

Payne Chapel African Methodist Episcopal Church, Nashville, Tennessee
Rev. Sidney Bryant, Pastor

The ministry of this congregation is based on a holistic approach and a determination to serve the physical as well as the spiritual needs of the church and community. The Living Breadbox is a service that provides emergency food and staple goods to individuals in need. Prison Outreach is a weekly worship service in the prison. On Target is a multimedia campaign that is designed to develop and broadcast messages promoting abstinence from alcohol and other drugs among African American males, ages 12-14. Payne Chapel sponsors Chi Rho Alpha, a group mentoring program for young men; Sister to Sister, an individual and group mentoring experience fostering positive development among young women; and Study Up—a tutorial program assisting young people in elementary through High School. The church has also established Project TEACH —Targeted Education for the African American Community Concerning HIV/AIDS.

Trinity United Church of Christ, Chicago Illinois
Rev. Dr. Jeremiah A. Wright, Pastor

A few of the social ministries of this congregation include an after-school Afrocentric training program for kindergarten and grades one through twelve that teaches reading, math, and computer science fifty-two weeks a year; a housing ministry focusing on both the homeless and rehabbing and purchasing HUD homes; senior citizens' Section 202 housing projects which provide housing for the unemployed, elderly, and the indigent; a ten-month Head Start program for unemployed and low-income families; a Day Care program; a feeding program; Alcoholics Anonymous; Narcotics Anonymous; "Free 'N One" Alcoholic Recovery Ministry; and a Prison ministry to men, women, and youth in the prisons in the Chicago metropolitan area. Trinity Church also has mentoring and Rites of Passage programs for African American youth, an Employment Ministry providing jobs for the unemployed and "unemployable", and a Legal Counseling Ministry to address the problems of the community and members of the church.

Windsor Village United Methodist Church, Houston, Texas
Rev. Kirbyjon Caldwell, Pastor

A few of Windsor Village's programs are: The Food Pantry which distributes non-perishable foods in conjunction with a program that offers vouchers for meals, a clothing resale shop that sells new and slightly used clothing for 15 cents to $15.00, an apartment ministry in which the congregation adopted a local apartment complex for outreach, and Operation Back to School that gives school supplies and two outfits to school aged children. In 1991 Operation Back to School served 1200 children. WAM, Windsor AIDS Ministry, offers food and case management to persons who are HIV positive. The Patrice House is a newly opened shelter for abused and neglected children that has a crisis nursery where persons may drop off children in times of crisis, spouse abuse, and so forth. The Imani School for Young Children is a private school for children beginning at three years of age through the fourth grade. Most of the programs of Windsor Village United Methodist Church are fully funded by its 6,000 members, and 99% of the persons served are not members of the congregation.

XII. Conclusion

In this document for dialogue across the Black Church and community, we have described the momentous crisis of our times—its dangers and opportunities. We have presented the position that what it means to be Black and Christian is one of the most critical questions we face as individuals and as an ethnic community and culture. We have acknowledged what some churches and communities are doing to concretize a Black theology of liberation today, and the present threat posed by the persistence of sexism, which is the result of the divide-and-conquer strategy of a racist and sexist society.

Throughout this discussion we have emphasized the pragmatic spirituality of the Black religious tradition that makes spirituality and social transformation inseparable. Black faith will not permit us to hide behind pious passivity and spiritualization of religion which make it an inward, private experience that has small consequences in the real world of power structures, social and economic decision-making, and electoral politics. We have implied throughout this paper that Black faith is a *working* faith—a faith that drives us out from our inward person to a outward behavior, from our prayer closets to our voting booths, from our personal bank accounts to our congregation's tithers' table, from Holy Communion to holistic community, and from the sanctuary to the streets.

There are many other things that we would like to say here, but we must leave them to the process of dialogue for exploration and decision. We would not, for example, neglect a macroscopic view that sees what it means to be Black and Christian in the light of centuries, continents, billions of faces on the planet, and God's ultimate purposes for all humankind. Our experience matches dramatically the experience of Israel in Egypt, Babylon, and Persia; harassed by the Seleucids and the Romans, and made exiles all over the world in a rejected diaspora for centuries. History has shown that any society will be different that has breathed the aroma of the Judeo-Christian ethos, because it automatically contains within it the seeds of its own radical self-correction and revolution.

America has the natural resources, founding ideals, and the vague outlines of a genuine humane community that is compatible with the biblical vision of the realm of God on earth. Our experience as African

American people makes us uniquely sensitive to the requirements of such a community and to the distant rumblings of that Realm coming in judgment and grace. To be Black and Christian in the United States is to work and pray for its consummation here in the land of our evolution as an African American people. But we work and pray not as though we were God's only chosen people with exclusive responsibilities and rewards for faithfulness, but on behalf of, and in community with, all the people of the earth.

We began with a call to make a decision between life and death, blessing and curses. We conclude with the same challenge. In Joshua 24 we see the closing of an era and God's call to another chosen people to make a profound choice about their faith for the sake of their future in a new era. There is the utterance of a divine litany that reminds this pilgrim people of the guiding hand of God, leading them from point to point, through their controversies to the moment when Joshua is to pass from the scene. Joshua, in his closing remarks presses God's issue of a new level of faithfulness that will be required in the new habitation of Canaan:

> Now therefore fear the Lord, and serve God in sincerity and in faithfulness; put away the gods which your foreparents served beyond the River, and in Egypt, and serve the Lord. And if you be unwilling to serve the Lord, choose this day whom you will serve, whether the gods your foreparents served in the region beyond the River, or the gods of the Amorites in whose land you dwell; but as for me and my house, we will serve the Lord. Then the people answered, "Far be it from us that we should forsake the Lord, to serve other gods; for it is the Lord our God who brought us and our fathers and mothers up from the land of Egypt." (Josh 24:14-17a)

Selected Bibliography

Akbar, Na'im. *Chains and Images of Psychological Slavery*. New Jersey: New Mind Productions, 1984.

Anderson, James D., and Ezra Earl Jones. *The Management of Ministry: Leadership, Purpose, Structure, Community*. New York: Harper & Row, 1978.

Baldwin, Lewis V. *There is a Balm in Gilead: The Cultural Roots of Martin Luther King, Jr.* Minneapolis: Fortress Press, 1991.

Bennett, Lerone. "The Crisis of the Black Spirit." *Ebony Magazine*, October, 1977.

Brueggemann, Walter. *Prophetic Imagination*. Philadelphia: Fortress Press, 1978.

Burrows, William R. *New Ministries: The Global Context*. New York: Orbis Books, 1981.

Burns, James MacGregor. *Leadership*. New York: Harper & Row Publisher, 1978.

Cone, James H., and Gayraud S. Wilmore, eds., *Black Theology: A Documentary History 1966–1979*. New York: Orbis Books, 1979.

Cone, James H. *God of the Oppressed*. New York: Seabury Books, 1975.

_____. *For My People: Black Theology and The Black Church*. New York: Orbis Books, 1984.

_____. *Martin and Malcolm and America: A Dream or A Nightmare*. New York: Orbis Books, 1991.

_____. *Black Theology of Liberation*. 20th anniversary ed. New York: Orbis Books, 1991.

Dionne, E. J., Jr. *Why American People Hate Politics*. New York: Simon & Schuster, 1991.

Dodson, Howard. "Review to Review." *The Witness* (March, 1978).

_____. "The Black Theology Project, 1983–1985: Goals, Objectives, Programs, Structures." New Public Library, Special Collections, Schomburg Center for Research in Black Culture.

Driver, Tom F. "Justice and The Servant Task of Pastoral Ministry." In *The Pastor as Servant*. Edited by Earl E. Shelp and Ronald H. Sunderland. New York: The Pilgrim Press, 1986.

DuBois, W. E. B. *The Souls of Black Folk*, in *Three Negro Classics*. New York: Avon Books, 1965.

Dulles, Avery. *Models of the Church*. New York: Image Books, 1974.

Fauset, Arthur Huff. *Black God of the Metropolis: Negro Religious Cults of the Urban North*. New York: Octagon Books, 1970.

Felder, Cain. *Troubling Biblical Waters: Race, Class, Family*. New York: Orbis Books, 1989.

_____, ed. *Stony The Road We Trod*. Philadelphia: Fortress Press, 1991.

Frazier, E. Franklin. *The Negro Church in America*. New York: Schocken Books, 1974.

Freire, Paulo. *Pedagogy of the Oppressed*. New York: Seabury Books, 1973.

Fluker, Walter. *They Looked For a City: A Comparative Analysis of the Ideal of Community in the Thought of Howard Thurman and Martin Luther King, Jr*. New York: University Press of America, 1989.

Groome, Thomas H. *Christian Religious Education: Sharing Our Story and Vision.* San Francisco: Harper & Row, 1980.

Harris, James. *Pastoral Theology: A Black-Church Perspective.* Philadelphia: Fortress Press, 1991.

Hessel, Dieter T. *Social Ministry.* Philadelphia: Westminster Press, 1982.

Hodgson, Peter. *Revisioning the Church: Ecclesial Freedom under a New Paradigm.* Philadelphia: Fortress, 1988.

Jones, Lawrence N. "The Black Churches: A New Agenda," *The Christian Century,* 96:14 (April, 1979).

King, Martin Luther, Jr. "Antidotes For Fear." In *Testament of Hope: The Essential Writings of Martin Luther King, Jr.* Edited by James M. Washington. San Francisco: Harper & Row, 1986.

Levine, Lawrence W. *Black Culture and Black Consciousness: Afro American Folk Thought from Slavery to Freedom.* New York: Oxford University Press, 1977.

Lincoln, C. Eric., and Lawrence H. Mamyia. *The Black Church in the African American Experience.* Durham: Duke University Press, 1990.

Lincoln, C. Eric. *The Experience in Religion: A Book of Readings.* New York: Anchor Books, 1974.

Marshall, Calvin B. "The Black Church—Its Mission is Liberation." *The Black Scholar* 2 (December 1970).

Matthews, Don E. "Black Women's Religion, History and Praxis: Implications for a Black Liberation Praxis." *Chicago Theological Seminary Register* 78 (Spring 1988).

Massey, Floyd, and Sammuel McKinney. *Church Administration in the Black Church Perspective.* Valley Forge: Judson Press, 1976.

Morris, Aldon. *The Origin of the Civil Rights Movement*. New York: Free Press, Collier Macmillian, 1984.

Myers, Linda J. *Understanding an Afrocentric World View: Introduction to an Optimal Psychology*. Dubuque: Kendall/Hunt Publishers, 1988.

Niebuhr, Richard H. *The Meaning of Revelation*. New York: Harper & Row, 1975.

Oglesby, Enoch H. *Ethics and Theology From The Other Side: Sounds of Moral Struggle*. New York: University Press of America, 1979.

Ogletree, Thomas W. "Dimensions of Practical Theology: Meaning, Action, Self." In *Practical Theology: Emerging Field in Theology, Church, and World*. Edited by Don S. Browning. New York: Harper and Row, 1983.

Paris, Peter J. *Social Teachings of the Black Churches*. Philadelphia: Fortress Press, 1985.

_____. "The Bible in the Black Churches." In *The Bible and Social Reform*. Edited by Ernest Sandween. Philadelphia: Fortress Press, 1982.

_____. *Black Leaders In Conflict*. New York: The Pilgrim Press, 1978.

_____. "Introduction to the Kelly Miller Smith Papers." In The Kelly Miller Paper Register, arranged and described by Marcia Riggs, Special Collections, Jean and Alexander Heard Library, Vanderbilt University, Nashville, 1989.

Poling, James N. and Donald E. Miller. *Foundations For A Practical Theology of Ministry*. Nashville: Abingdon Press, 1985.

Quinley, Harold E. *The Prophetic Clergy: Social Activism and the Protestant Ministers*. New York: John Wiley and Sons, 1974.

Roberts, J. DeOtis. *A Black Political Theology*. Philadelphia: The West-minister Press, 1974.

_____. *Black Theology in Dialogue*. Philadelphia: The Westminster Press, 1987.

Rooks, Charles S. *Revolution in Zion: Reshaping African American Ministry*. New York: The Pilgrim Press, 1990.

_____. "Toward The Promised Land: An Analysis of The Religious Experience of Black Americans." *The Black Church* 2:1 (1972).

Ruether, Rosemary R. *Liberation Theology: Human Hope Confronts Christian History and American Power*. New York: Paulist Press, 1972.

Smith, Archie. *The Relational Self: Ethics and Therapy from a Black Church Perspective*. Nashville: Abingdon Press, 1982.

_____. "The Relational Self In the Black Church: From Bondage to Challenge." In *Changing Views of the Human Condition*. Edited by Paul W. Prusyer. Macon, GA: Mercer University Press, 1987.

Smith, Kelley Miller, Sr. *Social Crisis Preaching*. Macon, GA: Mercer University Press, 1984.

_____. "Religion As A Force In Black America." In *The State of Black America, 1982*. Edited by James D. Williams. New York: The National Urban League, 1982.

Smith, Luther. *Howard Thurman: The Mystic as Prophet*. New York: University Press of America, 1981.

Sumner, David E. "The Local Press and The Nashville Student Movement, 1960." Ph.D diss., University of Tennessee, Knoxville, 1989.

Thurman, Howard. *Jesus and the Disinherited*. Richmond: Friends United Press, 1949.

_____. *Footprints of a Dream: The Story of the Fellowship of All Peoples*. New York: Harper & Row, 1959.

_____. *The Creative Encounter*. Richmond: Friends United Press, 1972.

Washington, Joseph R. *Black Sects and Cults*. New York: University Press of America, 1986.

Washington, Melvin James. *Frustrated Fellowship: Black Baptist Quest for Social Power*. Macon, GA: Mercer University Press, 1986.

West, Cornel. "The Crisis of Black Leadership." *America Magazine*. 1987.

Whitehead, James D. and Evelyn E. *Method in Ministry: Theological Reflection and Christian Ministry*. San Franciso: Harper Collins Publishers, 1980.

Wilmore, Gayraud S. *Black & Presbyterian: The Heritage and Hope*. New York: Anchor Books, 1974.

_____. *Black Religion and Black Radicalism: An Interpretation of the Religious History of Afro-American People*. 2d ed. New York: Orbis Books, 1984.

_____. "Origin and Future of The Black Theology Project: Some Reflections." *The Black Theology Project*. Special Collections, Schomberg Research Center in Black Culture, New York.

_____. "Black Theology and Pastoral Ministry." In *The Pastor as Theologian*. Edited by Earl E. Shelp and Ronald H. Sunderland. New York: The Pilgrim Press, 1988.

_____. "A Revolution Unfulfilled, But Not Invalidated." In James H. Cone, *A Black Theologian of Liberation*. 20th Anniversary ed.. New York: Orbis Press, 1990.

Wilson, Julius. *The Truly Disadvantaged: The Inner City, The Underclass, and Public Policy*. Chicago: University of Chicago Press, 1987.

Wimberly, Edward P. and Anne Streaty. *Liberation and Human Wholeness: The Conversion Experiences of Black People in Slavery and Freedom*. Nashville: Abingdon Press, 1986.

Index